A Living History Publi

Post War Blues

by Valerie A. Tedder

Dedication

For Sarah, my granddaughter, who frequently
asked 'What happened next?'.

By the same author

The Pantry Under the Stairs (1994)

Acknowledgements

The author would like to thank the following for
permission to reproduce photographs: Neville Chadwick
Photography; Mrs G. Coates; Leicester City Museums, The
Leicester Gas Museum; R. Pochin & Son Ltd; Mr S. Vernon,
Mr J. Zientek.

Published by Leicester City Council
Leicester City Libraries, Living History

Designed by Creativity Works

ISBN 1 901156 85 0

CONTENTS

Julie & me at Spinney Hill
Park. January, 1956.

Mum & Dad at De Montfort
Hall Gardens. August 1955.

Julie aged 2 years.

FOREWORD

My father, who had completed 18 years in the navy, was among the first servicemen to be demobbed following the end of the Second World War. Finding work was soul destroying as the factories and businesses were slow to change over from war to peace work. Father took what he could get, which was as a boilerman at a dye works. The fact that it entailed shift work and a bicycle ride of 16 miles a day did not deter him, but it was too much for Mother when she became pregnant. When the house next door to the dye works became vacant it seemed prudent to move house. It was the worst move of our lives.

The environment surrounding the house was horrendous with the daily output of noxious smells from unbleached and dyed wool, the stinking drains, the soot from the chimney and the dry dye dust that travelled on the wind and settled on everything. The wet washing and baby layettes were frequently covered in 'Technicolor' polka dots from the dye dust. Against this background the family worked hard to lead a normal life and to improve their lot.

This is the story of a young girl coming to terms with a changing world, starting life in a factory, and coping with adulthood against many domestic trials. The story is sad, humorous and heart warming as it reveals the strict supervision from a dominating mother and parents, who through no fault of their own, found no finances to improve their status. It gives an account of life in Leicester between 1946 and 1958: City were up for the Cup, television arrived, the Coronation, dancing at the Palais and trips to the cinema and theatres. Then there were the local bank holiday shows and day trips to the seaside. Woven into this local history, a young woman tries to carve out a future as a sample hand, have a social life of her own and the trials and tribulations of falling in love. After many years, driven to distraction by boredom, she makes a decision that changes her life forever.

Main picture: East Park Road in the 1940s. Imperial Typewriters Ltd. is on the left, Nottingham Road crosses East Park Road just behind the tram. (Leicester City Museums)

Right: Mum, Dad, Valerie and Julie in 1949 (V. Tedder)

CHAPTER ONE

1946 - Moving house

I disliked the house in Nottingham Road the moment I saw it. There was a depressing air surrounding it and it looked dark and dreary inside. An awful smell of wood, steel and wool stung the nose and its pungency remained with me for many years.

The mixture of smells came from three factories close to the house. As we stood in the street facing the house, there was Pollard Engineering Company just four houses away to the left. Next door and adjacent to the wall of our house, on the right, was the dye works of J.O. Wilson and Company Limited. Further down the narrow street and next door to the dye works was John Mason and Sons, the wood merchant. Our five houses were squashed in between these extremely busy industrial premises.

Nottingham Road was situated in the centre of a large, light industrial and engineering district. At the bottom of our street was East Park Road which housed the Imperial Typewriter Company, another dye works situated at the corner of London Street and Leicester Street, and a large shoe manufacturers opposite. In St Saviour's Road, at the rear of our homes, were the firms of Mellor Bromley, Gent's, and Rudkin & Laundon's. We were surrounded by busy factories, all emitting their own particular aroma and noise.

I wondered what had possessed my parents to move from our nice terraced house in Leopold Street, South Wigston, and later, when I was told the reason, I felt no better. I was only 11 years old and, of course, was not consulted over the move. When I saw number 57 Nottingham Road, a strange feeling of sadness and foreboding made me think that life was not going to be very pleasant in future.

My father had been in the Royal Navy for 18 years, which included his war service, and we were used to moving from flat to flat and house to house, to conform with his posting to naval ports, but this move in 1946 took some getting used to. Dad was tall, good looking, and I adored him. He had a brilliant smile and looked extremely attractive and smart in his uniform. I was forever boasting to my schoolmates of his travels abroad. What was I going to say about his new job when asked?

It was over a period of days that the explanation for moving was given to me. As I understood it, Dad had been among the first of the servicemen to be demobbed after the Second World War. Being one of the first in, he was first out. Unfortunately, he had difficulty finding work. The factories were slow to change over from war to peace work and many servicemen had been promised their jobs back after demobilisation. These men came first and Dad was not in that position after 18 years on the high seas. Some firms were reluctant to take on staff until the changeover was complete and the orders for work began coming in.

Dad, being a Chief Petty Officer, knew everything there was to know about boilers and engines, so he searched for work in this field. It had been his intention to branch out into something more intellectual and challenging, but it was too soon after the war ended to find suitable employment in a different occupation. He was forced to stick to the trade he knew.

When he was offered the job as boilerman at Wilson's dye works he gladly accepted it. He started at 6am,

Monday to Friday and Saturday mornings. It was necessary to start early to get up sufficient steam and hot water for the factory workers when they began their day at 8am. He found that the boilers were old and it took great strength shovelling the coal and coaxing the antiquated machinery into action. He used his wide experience to keep the boilers in good working order. Frequently, as the demand for dyed wool increased and extra coal deliveries were called for to cope with demand, he constantly requested the boss at the firm to replace crucial parts for the boiler, these in turn being out of date and hard to replace. In addition, because of the condition of the old boilers, Dad had the frequent and filthy job of cleaning and servicing them. It was rather worrying for him as he felt an obligation to keep the boilers in tiptop condition as the men in the dye works depended on him for their living. He should have received a higher wage for all his' skill and experience, but it was employment and to Dad that was the most important thing.

As time went on it became obvious that his employers did not appreciate or understand his work load. His loyalty and reliability appeared to mean nothing to them. His hours became longer and more awkward and eventually it became too much for Mother, as Dad seemed to be away from home more and more.

Mum and I lived quite happily in Leopold Street, a rented property, during the war years from 1939 to 1945. Dad had arranged the lease at the outbreak of war, when he was recalled into the service from being on the reserve, and in all those years he only stayed in the house when he was home on leave.

Unfortunately, when he obtained employment at Wilson's, the distance from South Wigston to Nottingham Road was about eight miles, a round figure of 16 there and back. Public transport was out of the question due to his unsociable hours, so he bought a second-hand bicycle and rode it to and from work daily.

When Mum became pregnant their tempers began to

fray, as Mother found herself being left longer and longer on her own. They argued loudly and seriously and, for the first time in my life, my beloved parents were constantly bickering and quarrelling. Mum began to get worried about her confinement with Dad being so far away and, when the house in Nottingham Road became vacant and was offered to them at a reasonable rent, it seemed the answer to a number of problems.

I did not want to move despite being told all the reasons and when I saw the house it immediately depressed me. I sulked for days. However, there was nothing to be done about it. So, in February 1946 we moved house. I knew we would live to regret it.

I had adored my little pink bedroom in Leopold Street. It had large sash windows that overlooked the rear gardens of our houses and those opposite. A beautiful lilac tree grew in the garden over the wall, and the long branches draped down over our side. When the petals dropped after blooming, a carpet of pale lilac spread out over our path and lawn and looked wonderful.

The house was old but sturdy. It had sheltered us during the air raids and shared the trying, anxious times of rationing and the horrors of war. We looked upon the house with affection. It was pre-war built, with no bathroom and an outside toilet. It was clean, private, quiet, and situated in a pleasant residential area.

It came as rather a shock when we moved to Nottingham Road, it was so totally different. The main outer wall of the new house ran the full length of the building from front to back and immediately behind it was the dye works factory. We could feel and hear the machinery and even the men shouting their instructions as they pushed and pulled the chains around the pulleys, as they heaved the large skeins of wool in and out of the bleaching and dyeing pans. Then came the swearing and shouting as they steered the large wooden skips on heavy iron wheels over the cobbled, uneven floor and the dips in the iron grills covering the drainage system that ran the full length and breadth of the factory.

Access to our house was through a large double gateway, with a small wicket gate set in the right-hand-side door. It was opened by turning a large metal ring and lifting the latch. The two large gates were held in place by great iron bolts, top and bottom. Our front door, which was hardly ever used, was on the right, then came two tall, thin windows at a corner followed by a large bay window and then the back door.

The kitchen was L-shaped and the small larder was used as the coal house. Every bag of coal delivered was carried in through the back door, around the kitchen and dropped inside the coal house. What a mess!

Opposite the coal house was a large window made up of small panes of glass. Outside, running parallel with the coal house, was the toilet. The kitchen window was given partial privacy by a six foot wooden fence erected to hide anyone going to the toilet. Unfortunately, the fence had been placed just the width of a paving slab from the window and it made the kitchen very dark.

Opposite the house and literally only the width of a lorry apart was a similar property to ours, with their doors and windows facing us. In addition, this property, occupied by an elderly couple Mr and Mrs Jackson for nigh on a lifetime, had a greenhouse built on the top of their flat roof over the kitchen. This too served to cut out our light. We discovered later that Mr and Mrs Jackson had lived in our house for a period, but had moved across the yard because it was a better property. Apart from the light obstruction I could never see any difference in either house or the outlook.

We had no garden, just the yard, with tatty window boxes around the bay windows. Nothing grew there. We tried various plants and even tomatoes in large pots but the air and bad light stunted growth and we had poor results.

Across the width of the yard at the bottom, near our kitchen, were double gates about six feet high, very old and dilapidated and more fencing at the sides which kept the factory private but gave access. However, it was not long before we discovered that the yard behind the gates was used for the deposit of the factory waste. One day, when the gates had been left open, we saw that the yard consisted of nothing but used and nearly empty dye drums. Large wooden, damaged skips were left to rot there and these in turn housed waste wool, in various stages of white: unbleached to bleached, dyed, failed dyed bundles and knotted spoilt skeins of wool. Many of these had been used to wipe down the oily and greasy machinery. Some of the drums contained the tiny grains of dye and when the lids were left off, the wind blew it everywhere like fine dust. In addition, there were wet and spoilt packages and brown paper. Tags, string, works invoices and work notes were strewn about the yard and many clogged up the drain. We saw sandwich wrappings and grease-proof bread paper that had been used for wrapping up pies and cakes, trapped in the various corners of the yard. With the gates securely locked, we were unable to see the rubbish tip just a few yards away from our back door and it was quite a shock when we discovered the health hazard. From then on, we kept a check on the mess by looking through the back bedroom window periodically. Dad did his best to keep it clean. We dreaded it when a visitor stayed with us and saw the view from the window.

Constant complaints to the boss, Mr Wilson, did little to ease the situation. He promised to speak to the men about it, but every couple of weeks it was as bad as ever.

The worst and most sickening of all, was the foul smell from the bleached or dyed, hot wool. The caustic soda and acid-based cleaners, used to sterilise the great steel vats and pans between the dying sessions, were extremely nauseating and hung in the air all the time.

Another pungent smell came from the drains, especially one near to our kitchen. The fence in the yard was erected directly above a large drain. This drain, with two thirds on the factory side and one third on ours, was covered with a thick iron grill. It was not long after moving in that my parents realised the health hazard from this neglected drain. The workers failed to clean it, being in the junk yard, so when the hot, sticky bleach or dye water came swirling down the pipe it gushed out and spilled over into our yard. The threads of wool and fluff quickly accumulated around the rough end of the pipe and the grill, soon blocking the drain. The filthy water frequently flooded over the paving slabs all the way to the back doorstep. It left an unsightly and smelly watermark when it dried. When the blockage was particularly bad and Mum could stand it no longer, she would rush around to the factory offices and demand to see the boss. She always threatened that if it was not cleaned out immediately she would inform the health authorities. Not once did Mr Wilson put himself out to inspect the mess. Usually, one of the factory workers was given the unpleasant job of drain cleaning. After he had poked it out with a stick and thrown down a couple of buckets of water, Mum or Dad would throw down a bucket of strong disinfectant. It was then left uncleaned on the factory side until Mother was obliged to complain again. My father, bless him, cleaned our side of this drain two or three times a week. He used a metal rod to stretch through as far as he could. The fluff, dregs and mess he placed on old newspapers and then burnt in the boilers.

And so, within a few weeks of moving house, we knew it had been a mistake. It was the start of an horrendous period in our lives, with constant battles against the dirt, soot, smells and health hazards. Mum dreaded the arrival of the new baby and the affect that our new living conditions would have upon us. She was determined that she would never give up looking for somewhere better to live. In the meantime, we soldiered on, with the tall, dark metal factory chimney standing guard close by and towering above us.

Back to basics

My next great disappointment was school. I had been attending a fabulous one named the Modern School on Little Glen Road, South Wigston. I had looked forward to attending it for a very long time and was settling down well. I was in the lowest form, due to the poor result of the eleven plus examination which I had taken at the age of ten in February 1945. I was bright enough, with lots of common sense, but the war had disrupted lessons, caused large classes and a shortage of teachers and, like thousands of other children at that time, I found education difficult and boring. Sitting at the rear of the class, because I was tall, also placed me out of sight. It was easy to crouch down behind the others and play about. So, with a small ring of friends similarly placed, we avoided the teacher's eye at every opportunity, paid little attention and spent most of our days dreaming. Most of my school reports placed me near the bottom of the class and most subjects had the words, 'Does not concentrate', 'Talks too much', or 'Could and must do better'. So the move to the new Modern School was to be an exciting beginning.

The school was aptly named being literally a modern building. I had never seen anything like it. The girls occupied the left side and the boys the right, with separate playgrounds. We were strictly chaperoned while on school premises and only associated with each other after school and outside the school gates. We wore a uniform which was just a long navy blue tunic, with box pleats back and front hanging from yokes that buttoned on each shoulder. The blouses were cream with long sleeves, and buttoned to the neck. My uniform was second-hand, purchased by my mother from one of her friends at the factory where she had worked during the war. It was kept until I needed it, then shortened and made to fit.

The Modern School had large, light classrooms, each one decorated a different shade of pale blue, green, fawn or beige. There was tiling of similar colouring half way up the walls. One wall of the classroom was all windows overlooking the playground and sports fields beyond.

The gymnasium, which was also the main assembly hall, was fantastic. There were climbing frames, vaulting boxes, exercise bars, and thick strong ropes hanging from the ceiling. There was a stage at the bottom end with dressing rooms on each side. The domestic science kitchen was marvellous, with the latest electric stoves and washing facilities. We girls were extremely eager to start the cooking classes. The boys had workshops equipped with all the latest tools for wood and metal work. Another wonderful thing for us girls was the toilet facilities and the shower rooms for after sport or gym. Albeit they were communal showers and some of us were a bit shy about running naked under the water jets, but it was a pleasure none of us had enjoyed before.

Then came the dining room, big and airy. After the rationing and school meals provided during the war, to have dinners of such variety was a great pleasure. We would eagerly queue up to receive our helping of food from ladies dressed in clean white aprons and wearing a type of mob-cap with all their hair pushed inside it. The kitchen sparkled with cleanliness and hygiene, with cooking utensils of shining steel and white crockery. This school was the tops and I was very shaken when I realised I would have to leave.

You can imagine how I felt when we moved and I had to go with Mother to try and get into another school. A week after we moved, arrangements were made for me and Mother to attend the Moat Girls School, situated just off St Saviour's Road. We had expected that I should be accepted into the school as the headmistress of the Modern School had indicated there was a place for me. No such luck. The head teacher at Moat Girls took one look at my last school report and said that I was below the necessary standard of education to attend. We were advised to try Bridge Road School further down the road.

Mother tried to explain things but she would not change her decision. Mother was extremely annoyed by the lack of understanding and the indifference shown by the education department.

The following day, when Mum had found out where Bridge Road School was, we dressed in best bib and tucker and presented ourselves at the school. When I turned the street corner and saw the school, I went into shock and sulked. I did not want to go there. It was an old fashioned school, squashed in between terraced houses in a residential area. There were no green fields. Inside, I felt it was claustrophobic, with small toilets and small cloakrooms, where the children's clothing was piled on top of each other through lack of space. The main hall had classrooms off to one side, which were dreary and dark. The walls were painted cream and all other paintwork a dark green. The electric lights were on most of the day whatever the season. The windows were set high up on the outer walls. The headmistress, an elderly woman, smiled graciously as she said that I was acceptable and could start straight away. I cringed. The times were 9am to 4pm, with no school dinners. I was allowed home at lunchtime from 12.15pm to 1.20pm. And that was that. Mother and I were escorted through the hall and, when we reached the last classroom on the left, Mother was gone. I was taken into a small classroom crowded with children, with two-seater desks very close together. The teacher frightened me instantly. She listened while the headmistress introduced me and the children stared as if I was from outer space. When the headmistress had gone I was told to stand in front of the class and to tell them all about myself. All 35 children sat still and upright in their seats as I stammered out my name and why I was attending their school in the middle of term. Twice I was told to speak up and then, when I had finished my little tale, the silence in the room for a few seconds made me want to cry in despair. I fought back the tears and sat down meekly in the seat indicated by the teacher on the front row, smack in front of her. She would move

me later, she barked out, when she had rearranged the seating.

I have never forgotten that first day. The teacher seemed overpowering, and it was noticeable how the children appeared to squirm in their seats before standing up to give the answer to a question that had suddenly been thrown at them. The teacher was tall, buxom and stood very erect. Her grey hair, taken back in a bun at the nape of the neck, was tight and stood out a little from her head. It was a smooth, tight bun and her hair scooped tightly back made her look very stern. She wore silver-rimmed spectacles, no make up, and was immaculately dressed in a blue frock with a white lace collar and a silver brooch between the points of the collar. Her voice was strong and boomed around the room. I discovered later she had been a hospital matron.

Eventually I was seated at a desk about halfway along the centre row but still directly under the beady eye of the teacher. I was thoroughly scared stiff and it took a long time for me to settle down. I hated my parents for moving and I was snobbish enough to think that it was a great comedown to attend Bridge Road School.

One good thing to come out of attending this school was the fact that I learned to swim. Once a week, in crocodile file through the streets, we were led to the Spence Street baths by the physical exercise teacher. We had been given dry runs in basic swimming strokes during gym class. Lying on our stomachs on the floor we made all the appropriate movements. After several weeks of this instruction we were ready to try them out at the baths.

When we were ready to enter the water, the non-swimmers were made to stand in line along the side of the pool. One by one we were allowed to enter the shallow water and stand in a row along the edge, performing the breast-stroke. Then, it was turn around, hands on the bar, and instruction on leg movements. It was hopeless trying to get the arms and legs to synchronise and frequently we sank to the bottom, coughing and spluttering. After a couple of weeks of this type of instruction, we were made to queue up on the side of the pool for a ride across the water on a belt. This was a canvas sausage-shaped bag, with tapes to tie it around our chest, and with a thick rope attached to pull the subject across the pool. We were lowered one at a time into the water and then, performing all the breast-stroke movements, were hauled quickly through the water. The teacher pulled us so quickly that the water under our chins built up a foam like a motor boat speeding along, and we were swamped over the head to nearly drowning. The fact that we knew we would be hauled up out of the water when we reached the other side, made us hold our breath and not panic too much. The belt was then removed from around us and quickly placed on the next child, who waited in the water while the teacher ran around the pool in order to repeat the process. We stood around in the water until all the non-swimmers had been dealt with. We had two such haulings in the three-quarters of an hour session.

Eventually, with no thanks to the teacher, I learned to swim under my own steam. Once this was achieved, and I had proved my worth, I received no further tuition. Together with other swimmers I spent the time swimming up and down the pool, keeping well away from the learners. All other strokes, back, crawl and butterfly, I learned by watching the more experienced swimmers. As for diving, I learned that the hard way by having many belly flops before getting it right. Anyway, it was enjoyable and lots of fun behind the teacher's back Our swimming lessons were held in the mornings between 9 and 10am. On the way back to school we were allowed a little leeway. Those first dressed were allowed to leave. There was a small bakery situated at the corner of Leicester Street and London Street, where several of us, with a penny to spare, could purchase a hot, freshly baked, crusty cob. We just had time to eat it and join the rest of the slowcoaches in the crocodile line back to school. It was a real treat and well worth waiting for.

'Keep the home fires burning'

Meanwhile, back at Nottingham Road conditions remained the same. Dad, now living on the doorstep to the factory, soon found he was called in to tend the boilers at all hours, Sundays and Bank Holidays. He helped with the removal of the delivered coal, dumped by the lorry drivers in the next gateway, to a better and safer storage space. There were various jobs that needed to be done within the factory between stoking up the boilers, so Dad was kept very busy one way or another.

Another chap named George Thorpe, who was employed in the factory as one of the dyers, assisted with the boilers when Dad had a day off or took his annual leave. He was quite a decent colleague to work with. He was small in stature and looked years older than his true age. He was round-shouldered and flat-footed. His boots were far too big and made him drag his feet. On his head he wore an old flat cap that had lost its shape and was stiff with grease and coal dust. Often he removed his false teeth when working and gave me a very gummy grin when he saw me. He was a nice chap, very conscious of the smell and dirt we had to put up with and always did his best to clear up any waste or coal dropped in our gateway. He looked a downtrodden working man and, in all the years I knew him, I never saw him with a clean face or decent clothes.

It did not matter what Dad or George did to keep down the smoke, it would pour from the top of the chimney that stood only a few yards from our house. The dark grey chimney was steel and looked like a single stack of cotton reels, and belched out dark sulphurous clouds of smoke and dust, constantly keeping an endless supply of hot water and steam for the factory.

The black soot spots settled everywhere and Mother

reached a stage where she refused to open any windows because of the constant film of coal dust along the window frames and sills. It was a battle to keep the house clean and the living room was dusted every day without fail. I know, because that was my job at lunch-time after I had finished my dinner and before racing back to school.

Despite the situation of the house in relation to the stretch of terraced properties, it was large and long. There was a front room, a large hall with a two-tiered staircase and a large whitewashed larder beneath. Then came the long narrow living room which was actually two rooms knocked into one, the kitchen and coal house. Upstairs, my bedroom was over the gateway and was always cold from the draught continually blowing through from below. Mum and Dad occupied the bedroom above the front room. Across the large square landing was the back bedroom which led immediately, down a step, into the small room converted into a bathroom. All the rooms, except mine, had a fitted fireplace built into the factory wall side of the house, which had been sorely neglected by previous

Queuing for coke at Aylestone Road gas works (The Leicester Gas Museum)

tenants. Bricks and rubble frequently fell down the chimneys, especially during high winds and with the various vibrations from the factory.

The only fireplace to be used regularly was the one in the living room near to the kitchen. The fireplace area was small compared to the wooden surround. It started with a large wide shelf above the fireplace, with two smaller shelves beneath. The wooden surround was about a foot wide each side to the floor. Between that and the black metal fire surround were fawn-coloured patterned tiles. Mother enclosed the area with a small black and brass fender. Above the whole fireplace, set into the frieze, was a large cupboard. Sometimes brick, soot and pieces of concrete found its way down the chimney, to drop unexpectedly onto the hot coals and shower cinders into the hearth or onto the home-made rugs. It was a wonder we did not have a house fire when the coal was suddenly struck and splintered out. It soon became impossible to have a decent fire because the draught was insufficient to make the fire burn properly and the peculiar shape of the chimney did nothing to help. It rose upwards from the grate for about eight feet, then across to the right for about ten feet, and then straight upwards to join the bathroom chimney and out into the tall chimney stack on the roof. A professional chimney-sweep had cleaned it prior to us moving in, but made it quite plain that he would not tackle the job again. It was so awkward and unsatisfactory that he refused to have the responsibility of failing to clean it properly because of the shape. Consequently, Dad purchased a set of brushes and rods and set about doing it himself. He had to clear the bottom half of the chimney first by pulling an old sack through on a rope, because the fixed rod and brush would not give in the bends. He then cut a hole about a foot square in the frieze to insert and operate the brush along the flat part of the chimney and to sweep the upper part normally. It enabled him to clean the three parts fairly well. When he had finished the job, he fitted a small door over the hole in the frieze and held it in place with a tiny butterfly nut. He always whitewashed over the door and the surround to get rid of the soot and dirt marks. It was a nightmare for him, a reluctant task he did only when absolutely necessary. After years of this unsatisfactory way of cleaning the chimney, he declared he would do away with coal fires and purchase an electric fire.

It was always a dirty job, fetching in the coal, smashing it up to fit the fire basket and cleaning out the ashes. We all looked forward to the day the electric fire arrived. In the meantime, we soldiered on. I recall one winter when there was a severe shortage of coal, and we were encouraged to burn old wood and coke to eke out the coal ration which had been imposed during the emergency. One night, Mum read in the local evening paper that the gasworks on Aylestone Road were selling two bags of coke per person on Saturday mornings. It had to be collected, there were no deliveries. Well, we needed fires, so I volunteered to fetch a couple of bags.

Mum covered a pram with an old curtain, handed me some cash and I set off. I walked all the way from Nottingham Road to the gasworks, queued for my two bags, which were loaded onto the pram, and walked all the way home again. It was a long way and my little legs felt very tired by the time I arrived home. It had taken me most of the morning to do the job. I repeated this trip twice more before the emergency was over and coal deliveries were resumed.

Then one day the fireplace, the coal, dirt and ashes, in addition to the constant chimney sweeping, aroused an anger in Dad that I had not seen before. He declared, 'No more. No more fires'. He went straight out and bought a beautiful, two-bar electric fire. Dad set about covering the whole of the fireplace with plywood, which he then papered, leaving a small gap at the bottom for the air to circulate. He placed the electric fire in front of the plywood surround and switched it on. It was marvellous. The room soon became warm and threw out more constant heat than ever the old coal fire did.

The electric fire was quite large with artificial coals laid in a black basket. The red bulb, screwed into a socket underneath, gave out sufficient heat to turn a small fan attachment. It gave the impression of a real fire burning as it slowly rotated causing a red and orange flickering. Across the front was a long steel strip with two bars running from end to end. The reflection of the two bars on the steel gave the impression there were four bars and deceived us into thinking there was more heat.

We had the electric fire for years and were never sorry it replaced the coal fire. When the artificial coals lost their blackness with constant dusting, Mum put black shoe polish on the top of each coal making it shiny and more lifelike.

Mum was very worried when we first had it because she thought it would bump up the electricity bill, and she forced us to be very economical. It was never left on when we were out and only switched on about half an hour before we were to sit down for the evening. In cold weather we were encouraged to continue wearing jumpers and cardigans in the home, to shut all doors and not waste electricity. As it happened, experience showed that we used no more electricity, moneywise, than burning coal and coke. It invariably worked out about the same.

I recall the cold, long winter evenings when we were able to undress before it at bedtime, or to get dressed by its warmth in the mornings. We thought it a godsend and that we should have had one years ago. I expect Dad had to wait until he had saved sufficient cash to buy one. That was usually the excuse for such delays in purchasing household items of this nature.

The fireplace at the far end of the living room, near to the hall, was only used at Christmas when we had a party. It was found to be rather expensive keeping two fires burning in the one room in the winter. This fireplace had lovely green and cream tiling down each side of the black metal surround. The black iron fire basket stood on legs

and was the largest in the house. There was a black marble shelf above it. Mum enclosed the fireplace on the floor with a brass fender which had two box-type seats attached. These seats, like stools, had dark brown leather tops and an ornate design engraved on the front panel. They slid onto the fender from the side. When the seat tops were lifted up there was room inside for wood, logs or coal. In our case we placed newspapers in one and brown wrapping paper and string in the other.

The fireplace in the front room was of similar design but again was only used at party time. The room was damp and eventually the tiles began to fall off and break, due to the dampness seeping through from the factory wall behind the fireplace.

The bathroom fireplace was a scream. It was extremely tiny, without a basket. I believe it was never intended to be used. It had a narrow black metal surround and a tiny narrow white enamel shelf above. Attached to the surround near the bottom were two black metal bars, obviously to keep in the coals but there was no attachment for a basket to be fitted. The entire bathroom floor was wooden. There was nothing metal or concrete beneath the fireplace bars to catch any hot burning ashes. Above the bars and set into the small chimney was a metal door with a ring in the centre. This circular door could be pushed back and up to allow smoke to escape up the chimney. When not in use the door was pulled forward and closed to keep the soot and draught out of the room. It was a shame we were not able to use this fireplace as in the winter the bathroom was the coldest room in the house.

The bath was excellent, a large one with a gas geyser supported on brackets above the taps. It did not take long to discover that the geyser was unsafe when it exploded a couple of times. On the last occasion we tried to use it, it blew up with a bang and Mum found herself without eyebrows. We decided it was too old and dangerous to use, so an application was made to the landlord for a replacement. It was never done. There was always some excuse for it not being replaced. At the time my parents could not afford to have the job done themselves. Consequently, we stopped using the bathroom and made do with stand up washes in the warmth of the kitchen.

As we had no inside toilet, Mum kept a beautifully clean white enamel bucket in the bathroom for emergency use during the night. There was no light and we kept a torch in the adjoining bedroom to find our way to the bucket if needed. However, it became a ritual most evenings to rush outside to the toilet before retiring.

In order to cut down on electricity and keep the living room warm, Mother purchased four grey, ex-army blankets and, using her treadle sewing machine, managed to make a huge curtain to stretch across the living room from one side to the other. It hung from a black iron pole that Dad acquired from somewhere in the factory. Large brass curtain rings were sewn along the top of the curtain and threaded onto the pole. Dad secured it each side with brackets screwed into the ceiling. It was so heavy that no draught came through it, but it was rather an unsightly colour. Over the years it wore quite thin where we constantly handled it to draw it across the room. When a hole appeared, Mother patched it. It certainly did what it was intended to do. When we drew it aside to go to the larder beneath the stairs for something, the change in temperature was very noticeable. In fact, the whole house was so cold that it became a habit to rush upstairs to collect night attire, run back down again, and undress in front of the electric fire. It was a pity we could not have had this luxury in our bedrooms. Mother's room, in particular, was so damp that tiny black spots appeared on the walls behind her dressing table, and clothes always felt cold and damp to the touch. Downstairs in the front room it was the same. Dad did his best to treat the walls with a damp course but it was a losing battle.

One day we had a power cut. All electricity in the house was off. Eventually, after numerous enquiries were made of the neighbours, it was discovered that we were the only house without electricity. When Mum checked the meter in the cupboard in the front room, she found it dripping with condensation. The boxes were streaked with white and droplets of water were seeping through the brickwork behind the meters. For several minutes Mum stared at the mess before her, then she touched it with her fingers. As she rubbed them together she could smell salt. Dad was summoned from the factory to make an inspection and for consultation. Immediately he knew what was causing the dampness. Behind the wall where the meters were fixed, in the factory, was a large wooden container. It had been purposely built to hold industrial salt used in the cleaning process of the vats between the dying sessions. The constant storing of the salt in this place over the years had caused the wood to rot, and the salt had corroded the wall and seeped through into our cupboard.

Mum went straight to the offices to report the matter to Mr Wilson. On this occasion he visited the house to see for himself and to make sure that what Dad had said had caused it was correct. However, Mother having proved her point that the situation was extremely dangerous and needed instant attention, Mr Wilson lost no time in contacting the electricity and gas boards. New meters were installed and, after consultation with the various inspectors, the wall behind them was treated with a special non-corroding paint. Mr Wilson paid for the new meters and had the wall treated. He reinforced the wall on the factory side and replaced the rotten wood on the container. There was never any suggestion that the salt container should be moved to another location. Anyway, despite the steps taken to make sure it did not reoccur, it soon deteriorated in the corners of the cupboard and along the skirting board on that particular wall. Our internal decoration was never the same as tiny black damp spots and damp patches frequently appeared and had to be dealt with instantly. It had been happening for so many years that it was all a waste of time.

My first kiss

My next move, when we had settled in, was to locate the nearest Sunday school. My parents, who always gave their religion as Church of England, did not discuss their faith. Dad only mentioned church parades in the navy, weddings and funerals. Mother appeared to have changed her views at some stage because, when I was about seven years old, she encouraged me to join the Church of Christ in Canal Street, when we lived at South Wigston. She gave no explanation, other than to state that the C. of E. were a load of canting humbugs and that she liked the spontaneity of the Church of Christ religion. So, with this in mind, I set off to locate the nearest such church to Nottingham Road, which turned out to be at the junction of Evington Road and Dashwood Road.

My first visit to this church took place on a wet Sunday afternoon. I was dressed in my Sunday best clothes, given two pennies for the tram fare there and back, and told to introduce myself. I was full of confidence riding the tram and entering the schoolroom for the first time. I had happy memories of the previous Sunday school, the anniversaries, Christmas concerts and parties, the summer outings and the harvest festivals, and expected this particular church to be run in the same vein. As soon as I walked in, I was accosted by one of the male teachers who bombarded me with questions about my name, address, parents, school and previous religious undertakings. I was a little afraid and wondered what I had let myself in for. When he was satisfied that I was a genuine customer, he led me through to the main body of the church and told me to sit down quietly next to several boys and girls of similar age. After a few hymns and a short sermon, we were split into small groups and moved to the seats at the side of the church. Here we received further instruction. Half an hour later we returned to the main part of the church for the final hymn and prayer, during which the collection plate was handed around. I felt in my pocket and dropped my one and only penny onto the plate. I felt I had been made welcome and promised to return the following Sunday afternoon. I walked home, my return fare having gone into the collection plate for a good cause.

From then on, I attended regularly until the age of 23 years. In fact, I was in the bible class for well on six years. You reached a status in special bible tuition at the age of 18 when, if you decided, you could be baptised into the church. I never made that decision, and by the time I was 23 I had changed my career and views on religion. It eventually led me to stop attending church altogether except, like my parents, to attend weddings and funerals.

However, I admit, those years at the Church, getting involved in the activities and social events, were very happy and interesting times. I recall with fondness the Sunday school anniversaries, with me taking part in the choir and, on occasions, reading or singing solo. One of the Church Elders was a Mr King, a stout man, always smartly dressed. He had a shiny bald head and wore spectacles. He was very strict and knew how to get the best out of the choir. It was fascinating watching him conduct, swaying, lost in his music, but coaxing the best from each member of the group. Any event he was in charge of was always successful as far as the choir was concerned.

It was the same at Christmas, when we practised every Sunday evening after service in readiness for the carol services and the Christmas Eve carols that were performed in the street outside the home of everyone who requested a visit. However, Mr King's seriousness did not stop the usual antics of the children - playing about, dropping hymn books and singing out of tune - just to see him get annoyed. It was not like day school, because he was unable to do much more than stop us from taking part in the events.

Then came the harvest festivals, splendid occasions when everyone tried to outdo their neighbour by presenting for display the finest fruit, vegetables, flowers, bottled fruit and jams. A table placed at the rear of the church was always laden with produce brought at the last moment or actually to the harvest service. The church looked a picture when completed, and the large pillars each side of the church were draped with beautiful flower garlands. The altar was covered with the whitest of white linen table cloths and in the centre, propped up so it could be clearly seen, was a freshly baked loaf in the shape of a sheaf of corn. It must have been two feet high and looked magnificent. Surrounding it, in a patterned display, were vegetables and fruit. Everyone was encouraged to donate something, and I remember one year someone sent tins of fruit and vegetables, which raised an eyebrow or two, until it was explained that it was all God's fruit of the earth, no matter how man presented it.

When Dad had his allotment, he chose the best parsnips and carrots, or potatoes and kidney beans, for me to take. Whatever it was, Mum would wash it and scrub it clean. When Dad was obliged to give up his allotment, I was sent to purchase fruit from the greengrocer's shop. It was usually apples, which Mum washed and polished until they shone like glass. I would watch proudly as my gift was displayed among all the rest.

The only times I recall my parents attending the church were on the occasions of the harvest festivals and the Sunday school anniversaries. There were odd times when I had been chosen to speak a verse or two from the bible or sing a short solo at some special church function, when Mum would attend to listen and give me support, but she never stayed to converse with any member of the congregation afterwards.

The church was one that catered for families, but many of the Elders in charge were very set in their ways and failed to move with the times. Services became too routine and repetitious. Even a young couple, who took over the ministry on their return from overseas, found great difficulty in bringing modern ideas into the church. It was only after a number of the Elders died and their places

were taken by a younger set, with a more modern thinking towards Christianity and the way the church should be run, did it manage to survive and attract younger people. Years later, I learned of a split in the congregation, when several members left and joined the United Reformed Church.

However, during my teens I was quite happy to go along with the church routine as it was. I well recall that, prior to the Sunday evening service, our small group of six boys and six girls met in the schoolroom to exchange news, then crept quietly into the church to sit on the back two rows, just inside the door. Here we would speak in whispers and hand around sweets. Frequently, one of the group would be asked to take round the collection plate and, being at the back, no one noticed how small our donation was.

After the service we would hold a conference to decide where we would take our walk that night. During the summer months it was our habit to walk from the church to one of the parks - Evington, Victoria or Spinney Hill. Our favourite place was Piggy's Hollow, a heath or common land in Evington village. There were many old trees and plenty of grassland to sit on and talk. It was on one of these visits to Piggy's Hollow that I received my first adult kiss. Before this, any kisses I had received had always been a peck on the cheek.

The group seemed to pair off into couples but I and another youth, very tall, dark and bespectacled, stayed our solitary selves. We were friends but did not hit it off sufficiently to be classed as a couple. Among the remaining youths was one who was very attractive, with curly, light brown hair, shining eyes and a brilliant smile. He was softly spoken and very polite towards the girls. In addition, he appeared very worldly wise and could hold a good conversation. He had a carefree attitude that appealed to us, and he seemed to drive us wild because we wanted to be in his company, listening to his every word. He became leader of the group and we were all happy to follow his lead. There was one girl in the group that he was very interested in, so we kept our distance, hanging around them just in case he tired of her, or her of him. We secretly wished he would date us but were too shy to impart these thoughts out loud. Although I liked him, having a boyfriend was out of the question for me. I was totally at a loss to think what I should do if I happened to meet a fellow that interested me sufficiently to date. Everyone was well aware of my mother's views on having boyfriends and she was very strict on where I went or with whom. I was always the first person to leave the party to get home on time. Even after the Sunday evening walks, which were innocent enough, I had to allow enough time to get home by the stated hour. Often, I ran all the way home if I miscalculated the time. Mum never accepted an excuse. As I did not possess a watch, I relied heavily on others for the correct time. I was quite a popular teenager, but Mum's strictness was a great drawback as far as my socialising was concerned.

I recall the evening of that first kiss quite clearly. It was something to remember. We were sitting in a circle on the grass at Piggy's Hollow, when the lads started a conversation about film stars and the kissing sessions. This drifted into the lads joking about kissing the girls in the present company. Before we knew it, our attractive leader had been challenged to kiss all the girls and report back on who was the best. Techniques were discussed. We girls were shy and embarrassed and flatly refused to participate in such a stunt to satisfy their whim. Before I knew it, our leader had accepted the challenge and grabbed the girl sitting nearest to him - me. He wrapped his arms tightly around me, swung me backwards and gave me a kiss on the mouth. I thought it was most passionate. When I came up for air, full of embarrassment, I did not know what to do with myself, or what to say. I protested loudly when I regained my senses. I blushed as the lads sent up a cheer and encouraged him to try another girl. Too late, before he could grab hold of the next one, the girls were up on their feet and hedging away as fast as possible. They began to disperse to avoid any further attempts.

It was all very innocent and apart from feeling embarrassed, nobody seemed to be bothered. I avoided his eye contact for a few weeks but still went along with the group for the Sunday evening walks. Eventually the mad session was forgotten, except by me. Well, everyone remembers their first kiss, surely.

CHAPTER TWO

The 'Technicolor' layette

Julie, age 2 years
(V. Tedder)

Mother, at the age of thirty five, was about four months pregnant when we moved. Just like when she was carrying me, she did not look pregnant until about seven months. She was so slender and only five foot four inches tall. I remember the day that she told me about it. I was invited into her bed and informed that I should soon be having a brother or sister. I cut her short by saying that we had been told all about babies in the biology class at school and she had nothing to worry about. My knowledge of babies was nil but I thought I knew it all at the time. Mother accepted what I said and from then on any bothers she had during pregnancy she did not hide from me.

I thought it was a wondrous thing to happen and could barely wait for the baby to arrive. I felt her tummy and the baby moving. It filled me with such interest and, in readiness for its arrival, I began knitting matinee coats and sewing tiny dresses.

Mum booked into Bond Street Maternity Hospital which came under the control of the Royal Infirmary. At each visit she paid an amount of cash towards the fourteen pounds confinement fee. After 12 years this was only an increase of three pounds on the fee paid at the Royal Naval Hospital in Gillingham, Kent, where I was born. We laugh when we think how we were both purchased on the weekly.

Unlike the system today of having blood tests and scans during pregnancies, there was no such strict checking of mothers at that time and Mum went to the maternity home once a fortnight for a minor check up. She hoped she would give birth to a small baby like me. I was full term, but weighed in at four pounds and fourteen ounces. Nowadays any child weighing less than five pounds is automatically placed in an incubator under supervision and observation for a time. There were no such contraptions in 1934. Mum, worried about my weight, consulted the matron. She reasoned that it was sufficient weight to carry during pregnancy and to give birth to, and that if she had her way, no mother would have a child weighing more than six pounds. They had all the world in which to grow. So, with the matron's views still in her mind, Mother was not too concerned when she continued to look so slim during her pregnancy.

The cot that I had used, a brown wooden one with a drop side, had been taken apart and stored. It was brought out, dusted and reassembled. Then it was placed in Mother's room and a new mattress purchased. Mum became very busy machining numerous pieces of sheeting to fit the cot, together with pillowslips and satin-edged blankets. She spent hours embroidering satin pillow covers and small eiderdowns to fit the pram.

When it came to buying the pram, I questioned her relentlessly on the size and design. I wanted a size that would accommodate me when I took the baby out for walks. Eventually, Dad made the decision for us. He chose a suitably sized pram that was for sale in a local shop. It had a black hood and apron, and let down at the front in a pushchair style. I was allowed to push it up and down the gateway numerous times to get used to it. I felt so proud, even though it was empty. Each time the pram was taken out of the house it went via the front door. It was manoeuvred with skill in and out and, when not in use, was parked in the living room behind the great grey curtain.

Mother prepared me over the months of her pregnancy for the two week absence from home. She taught me the rudiments of simple cooking and instruction on housework and washing. I was to look after Dad and the house in her manner of doing things, and I was to take my responsibilities very seriously. She instilled in me the seriousness of running a home as an adult would, and nothing, absolutely nothing, was to go wrong. As it later transpired, her expert tuition paid off and I became quite a talented housekeeper.

Suddenly, the baby was due, announcing its arrival during the early hours of the morning on 8 July. Unfortunately, it could not have happened at a worse time. Dad was busy in the boiler room getting up steam for the factory. It was Monday morning and, after a shut down for the weekend, the boilers could not be left, needing constant monitoring of the gauges. Dad sent for his relief, George Thorpe, but was reluctant to leave the premises until he arrived. As time went by, Mum became very anxious and feared she would give birth at home. The taxi arrived at 7am and waited, just as Dad waited for George. Unable to hold on any longer, Mum stated her intention of leaving and went to the taxi. Dad was worried to death. Mum needed him but he did not want the boilers blowing up for lack of supervision. I heard them arguing. Mum shouted something like, who was more important, her or the bloody boilers. Dad helped her into the taxi just as George arrived on his bicycle. A wave of the hand was sufficient for the hand over.

Later, Mum told me that she thought she was going to have the child in the taxi as she crossed the Clock Tower, but she managed to hold on, eventually giving birth in the

bathroom at the maternity home while she was still partly dressed.

It was a girl, arriving about 8am and weighing in at 6lbs 2ozs. She was a gorgeous, perfect child but with rather yellow skin. Within minutes of the birth she was diagnosed Rhesus and whisked away in the arms of a nurse to the Leicester Royal Infirmary. Mother thought she was dead because it happened so quickly. At the Infirmary the baby underwent a complete blood change. Dad, on his bicycle, first visited the Infirmary every evening on his way to see Mum at Bond Street. I recall every bulletin saying the baby was doing well and recovering. Dad said that she was propped up in a cot by ten tiny pillows. She had rosy cheeks and slept most of the time. The nurses on the ward thought she was a delightful baby and constantly attended to her needs.

It was thought she would not recover from such a major blood transfusion and, when the hospital padre visited Mum to request a name so that he could baptise the child in case she died, Mum was frantic for a time. She agreed on the name of Julie and the baby was so baptised. Despite reassurances from the nursing staff and from Dad, Mum did not believe that her baby was still alive until she was returned to her five days later. Julie was quite a celebrity, being the first Rhesus baby born at Bond Street Maternity Hospital to survive.

In those days, children were not allowed to visit maternity homes, so I resigned myself to seeing Mum and the new baby in two weeks' time. However, Dad had an idea. One afternoon he arranged for us to travel into Leicester on the tram. I saw Mum all right, but not from inside the hospital.

Bond Street Maternity Hospital looked like a row of terraced houses, with straight flat windows and a small window sill, just wide enough to stand on, on tiptoe. Dad lifted me up when he had located the room Mother was occupying, and he held me around the waist while I peered into the window and waved to Mum. She mouthed that it was nice to see me and asked if I was being a good girl, but we could not hear one another. I then waited patiently on a seat in the entrance hall while Dad paid his half hour visit. When we left I was treated to another look through the window to wave goodbye. Dad arranged a similar visit the following week but I did not see my sister until she came home with Mum 11 days later. What a smashing child she turned out to be - a lovely round face, pale skinned with natural rosy cheeks, big blue eyes and fair curly hair. The exact opposite to me when I was born, except for the eye colouring. As she grew older she retained the wonderful fairness of skin but her hair gradually lost its curliness. By the time she was two years old the only remaining curls were two ringlets down the back of her head. It seemed such a shame. My hair had been as straight as a poker from birth and I envied Julie's curls. It was sad when they grew out and her hair became as straight as mine.

Having a new baby in the house was most exciting but everything was suddenly topsy-turvy. Julie, a good child during the day, cried a lot during the night and we had many interrupted nights. I quickly learned how to change nappies, care and feed her, and took my turn with Mum and Dad during the night to tend to her. Sometimes she cried so much, and disturbed Dad, that Mum picked her up and took her downstairs, strapped her safely in the pram, and left her there to cry herself to sleep. Dad needed his rest because he had to be up so early and had a lot of responsibility tending the boilers.

Nappies were the biggest problem at that time. There were no packs of disposable nappies available and we had to make do with home-made. Mum purchased several yards of soft white terry towelling and made about fifty napkins on her sewing machine. All were beautifully hemmed and then washed to take out the newness and make them really soft. When they were dirty or soiled, they were soaked in a white enamel bucket, placed under the kitchen sink, for at least a day, before being transferred

to a galvanised bucket which was placed on top of the gas cooker and the contents boiled. Usually, when the napkins were hung outside on the line, they were covered in tiny soot specks before they were dry. We became quite used to re-washing garments. Things came to a head one day when Mum lost her temper after discovering what had happened to the washing on the line and to Julie, asleep in her pram outside the back door.

As the drying of washing depended a great deal on the weather, Mum was very anxious to take every opportunity when the weather was good. On this particular day, an excellent sunny drying day, she had started early in the morning to complete a heavy wash of sheets, pillowcases, towels, napkins and baby clothes. A few hours later, when the washing was nearly dry, it suddenly clouded over and threatened rain.

Julie was about seven months old at the time and was in her pram in the yard, fast asleep. She was dressed in a hand-knitted white layette and her pram covers were white and pink silk. Mum was inside the house completing her household chores when she noticed that it was getting darker and had started to sprinkle with rain. She ran outside to check on Julie and fix up the pram cover and hood. What she saw then made her see red. The beautiful pram covers and Julie's new layette were covered in tiny multicoloured specks. She ran with the pram under the gateway, out of the rain, and went back to check on the washing. It was the same. Instantly she knew what had happened. The wind, prior to the rain, had blown the fine dye dust from the drums and floor in the factory yard and it had settled everywhere. The damp washing, together with the rain spots on Julie, had left tiny multicoloured polka dots. Even her face had coloured spots from where the dust had settled and then the raindrops. Mum was so cross she picked up Julie, placing her under one arm, and a bundle of damp washing pulled from the line she put under the other. She marched straight round to the offices in the factory and demanded to see Mr Wilson.

The King and Queen at the Imperial Typewriter Co., 1946 (Mrs G. Coates)

It was a bad time. The boss was busy with representatives and quickly agreed to look into the matter when he was free. Mum lost her temper with him, told him what she thought of him and his factory, and returned home to re-wash the laundry. Julie was changed and her face sponged clean.

About half an hour later there was a knock on the back door. The boss had sent one of his factory employees with a tub of powdered bleach so that Mum could do her washing in this special dye removing powder. It was an industrial bleach and not at all suitable for the delicate babywear or household fabrics. Mum was none too

pleased. She refused the powdered bleach and told the employee to tell the boss that she would use her own method to clean the washing. His job was to make sure it did not happen again.

She eventually removed the dye by soaking everything in a bucket and using her own light bleach. Then it was back to boiling everything in the bucket on the stove, followed by hand turning the small mangle. It was extremely hard work. As for the silk pillowcase and pram cover, it took a long time to fade out the coloured spots. Soaking them in bleach would have ruined them altogether. Mum never forgave the boss for his cold, callous attitude about the matter. Dad was scared in case Mum had gone too far in her temper tantrum and we were asked to leave. I don't think the boss cared much whether we were there or not. Unfortunately, there were several occasions over the years when a similar incident occurred, but it was never quite as bad as the day when Julie's lovely new layette was transformed to an amazing 'Technicolor'.

Not long after the birth of Julie, in October 1946, there was great excitement at school when the news spread that Leicester had been chosen to be visited by King George VI and Queen Elizabeth. We knew all about them and the two princesses because of their wartime visits to the Services and the bombed-out areas of London. Frequently their photographs were in the newspapers, especially when they were on tours and visits around the United Kingdom. The proposed visit to Leicester sparked off new interest at school and we were reminded of the royal duties and had a re-cap on the successors to the throne. By the time the day arrived, 30 October, we were ecstatic with enthusiasm.

They were very popular and we were all very patriotic royalists. The *Leicester Mercury* published a map of the route and a list of the places to be honoured with a royal visit. Among them was the Imperial Typewriter factory on East Park Road, just at the bottom of our street.

The royal route was highly decorated everywhere with flags and bunting, and outside the Imperial Typewriter works was no exception. A flag, or something red, white and blue, fluttered from every window. At the front entrance to the factory there was a massive array of flowers. The whole area was a blaze of colour. Even Mum, with her house situated halfway along Nottingham Road, flew the Union Jack from a pole lodged in her front bedroom window.

About an hour before the royal party arrived, I managed to find a small gap at the front of the crowd that had gathered along the kerb opposite to the factory entrance. When the royal party arrived, I saw nothing but the backs of their heads as they were shepherded from the cars, up the steps and inside the factory.

We waited patiently. Sometime later a roar went up from the crowd as people noticed that the distinguished visitors were beginning to emerge from the door. Then, side by side, standing on the top step facing us, I saw the King and Queen for the first time. I was dumbstruck. It was such an emotional moment. Immediately I saw how small in height the Queen was, but how beautiful. She smiled and acknowledged the crowd with the famous royal wave. The crowd began cheering and the noise was deafening. I watched unable to speak through excitement. I was actually seeing them in real life. What a day for me. A moment or two later, they walked down the steps and re-entered the waiting car. It had been well worth the wait, the pushing and shoving to get a good position, and the screeching, deafening noise of the cheering. It was an event I have never forgotten.

Down on the allotment

Shortly after we moved to Nottingham Road Dad decided that, as we had no garden, he would look around for an allotment. He thought it would be good for us to get away from the house and environment two or three times a week, and the produce he could grow would subsidise our small income.

Eventually, he heard there were several allotments for rent at Crown Hills on Coleman Road, and applied to the appropriate allotment committee. He was given an allotment for a nominal rent and, although neglected by the previous tenant, as soon as the weeds and grass were removed he found the soil was not too hard to turn and work. Starting work early in the morning meant he finished early and could get onto the allotment during the afternoons and early evenings. Within a few months Dad had transformed it. He found that the previous gardener had set blackberry, gooseberry, redcurrant and blackcurrant bushes that only needed a trim to produce good crops. Also, Dad found many roots of cottage garden flowers, pinks and carnations when the weeds were cleared, and these too gave an ample supply of flowers for Mum's table during the summer months.

On fine days, when I arrived home from school, Mum would pack a bag with a flask of tea and a few sandwiches and cake. Pushing Julie in the pram, we would walk to the allotment to spend a couple of hours in the fresh air. I was allowed to potter about helping Dad by doing odd jobs

Julie on Dad's allotment
(V. Tedder)

under his instruction. Julie, with a small bucket and spade or a piece of stick, would play happily digging into a small plot of soil especially set aside for her. Mum did very little, picking some flowers, or watering plants that needed it. She usually sat on an old chair supervising Julie. About 5pm we would stop our work for tea. The jam sandwiches tasted great.

Sometimes, on a very hot evening, when we had finished on the allotment and washed ourselves clean, we would call in at the Crown Hills public house. Sitting outside in the yard I would have a lemonade, shared with my small sister, and Mum and Dad would have a glass of what they fancied. Then it was straight home to bed. My bedtime was around 9pm, after Julie had gone to sleep.

When Julie was about two years old, Dad fixed a small seat and foot rests to his cycle so that he could take her to the allotment more frequently. It was also quicker and easier getting her there and back. One day he returned home laden with garden produce. He removed Julie from the seat and let her run ahead indoors to Mum. He then took off the garden produce tied to the little back-carrier behind the saddle and other vegetables tied onto the handlebars. He propped the cycle against the window boxes while he carried everything into the kitchen. When he returned a few seconds later to lock the cycle up for the night, he saw it being ridden out of the open gateway by a young man. From the rear he looked in his twenties. Dad shot off in hot pursuit and, although he chased the culprit for a street or two, he was unable to catch up with him. Dad was most upset. The theft was reported to the police but the cycle was never traced. Dad could not afford to replace the cycle, so from then on he walked to the allotment carrying Julie on his shoulders when she was tired. The bicycle was a very old type which Dad had specially adapted to carry a small child, as stipulated by law. We could not see what use the young man would get by stealing it.

Dad rented the allotment for many years and it gave us much pleasure and a great amount of good fresh produce. He was a good gardener. When he later had thrombosis of the leg and was advised to give up the heavy work of gardening, Julie and I worked it for about three years. Then our circumstances changed and we were forced to reluctantly give it up. We sorely missed the fresh vegetables and fruit. Buying them from the shops was never the same, and they always seemed to taste differently, we thought.

'Be Prepared'

After a few months at Nottingham Road, I realised I was without a special friend. There were plenty to associate with in school but once home I found none in the vicinity. My nearest schoolfriend lived on the far side of St Saviour's Road, and others lived in the Green Lane Road area. I had numerous boys and girls to play with at Leopold Street, but since moving I discovered my evenings and weekends were quite lonely. Apart from the Sunday school hour, I amused myself reading, sewing and caring for my sister. Jobs in the home increased and I became a second mum.

One Sunday, after the lessons were finished, I was approached by a Miss Guthins, who was the leader of the Girl Guide pack at the church. She asked if I would like to attend the meetings held once a week in the church schoolroom. She explained that they met for about an

hour and a half and, in addition to earning badges, played games, had outings, attended different church parades and went camping once a year in the county. It all sounded interesting and exciting and I could not wait to get home to ask permission to go. It was not as easy as I thought. My parents, although agreeing it was a good idea, felt uneasy because it meant travelling on the tram there and back, and would mean having to go during the winter months when it was dark in the evenings and not safe for a young girl my age to be out and about alone. Eventually they agreed, but certain arrangements had to be made first.

On the first evening Mother went with me. The tram stopped on Evington Road just a few yards from the church, but on the return journey I had to cross the main road. We met another lady who assisted the guide leader, named Jean Hull, who told us she had to cross the main road herself in order to walk home. She agreed to wait with me at the appropriate stop and to make sure I got on safely. Dad or Mum would then wait at the other end for me to get off. By the summertime, I was able to do the journeys alone and often walked home, but I never told my parents.

The evenings spent with the guides were great. I thoroughly enjoyed myself. I felt quite proud when I was sworn in and given my badge. I wore it on my blouse for months until Mother could afford to purchase a uniform. The only event that I was excluded from through lack of uniform was a church parade, but I always attended as an onlooker.

Before long, I was informed that one of the older guides was leaving and that her uniform was available. She was about my size and only wanted five pounds. I was over the moon with excitement. At last, I was to be one of the group. I took the uniform home for my parents to see. It consisted of a blue dress, a brown leather belt, a red kerchief and a navy blue beret. The dress, beautifully washed and pressed, had originally been a dark blue, but had faded with wear and washing. It had a high neck with a collar, silver buttons down the front and on the breast pockets, and long sleeves. There were a number of dark circles on the sleeves where badges had been removed. The fact that the dress looked well worn pleased me. I did not look like a new recruit in it. The belt was highly polished and the metal buckle had the words 'Be Prepared' engraved upon it. The red kerchief was fine but the beret had been washed so many times, and been out in the rain, it had shrunk and lost its shape. However, it was a uniform and I was well pleased. I did not for one minute object to it being second-hand.

Mum was satisfied it was a good purchase and the following week I went in full uniform and paid the leader the money. From then on, I volunteered for everything. I even managed to get chosen to carry the flag at a special event held at St Philip's Church on Evington Road. I recall it was a very windy day and I had great difficulty controlling the flag as it swayed. With the end of the flag-pole slotted into a small brown leather pouch attached to my belt, the weight and the swaying made the contraption gradually push downwards and I was constantly having to let go of the flag-pole to hitch up the belt to my waistline. It took great skill handling the flag and I dare not let a hand relax for one second.

The outings, usually on a Saturday, were out in the county. I remember a visit to Saddington Hall where we were given tea and cake and allowed to roam at will in the well cared for gardens. Then there were trips to the museums in Leicester and the Castle Gardens. Sports and picnics in Bradgate Park and Abbey Park were marvellous. We coped in all kinds of weather.

We paid a small subscription each week towards the trips. In the winter months we spent the evenings learning first aid, knots, Morse code, mapping and orienteering in readiness for the summer camp. My sleeves soon held many badges as I passed each test in succession.

Then the most exciting thing happened to me for a long time. I was chosen, with five others, to go camping. It was for one week during the school holidays. The campsite was situated at Woodhouse Eaves in the grounds of The Brand belonging to Lt.- Colonel Sir Robert Martin. I agreed to go before seeking permission from my parents. When I arrived home with the consent form, Mother at first refused. When she learned it was not going to cost a fortune, she signed. The accompanying letter stated that everything was provided, including transport. All I had to do was to make sure I packed everything in the personal line that was listed. In addition to clothing, wellington boots and underwear, I had to provide myself with an enamel mug, a plate and cutlery with my name on. About a month before, we were given a new type of kitbag with a draw-string fastening in which to pack everything. All garments, with my name tags patiently sewn into each one, were folded and packed into the kitbag. The crockery and cutlery had narrow elastoplast strips with my name on, either stuck on the bottom or wrapped around the handles. This method was not such a good idea. After a few days wear and washing, the ink faded and the elastoplast went black and sticky with the cotton pieces fraying along the edges.

The week before going to camp, the guide group spent the evening being instructed on behaviour and what was expected of us, like sharing the chores around the camp. A daily rota was to be posted in the large mess tent so that we knew exactly what we had to do that day. Although waterproof ground sheets were provided, bedding was not. Those fortunate enough to possess sleeping bags were encouraged to take them, neatly rolled and tied to the kitbag. Those without such a luxury, which included me, were to take a single sheet and a blanket, similarly rolled tight and attached to the kitbag. Mum sorted out a white Whitney sheet and a dark green blanket. Both were rolled inside clean but old curtain material to keep them clean during transit.

When the great day arrived Dad took me, in my smartly pressed uniform, with my kit on the tram to the church schoolroom. There were a large number of guides waiting at the church, all in uniform but with their own particular coloured kerchief. I made friends with a guide from St Philip's Church pack and we were inseparable all week.

There was such a scurry and a flurry as we loaded up. The tents and camping gear were already loaded into a large van. We were instructed to sling our kitbags into a smaller van, then wait to be allocated a seat in a car. When all was ready, we climbed into our designated transport and left in convoy for Woodhouse Eaves.

On our arrival there was much excitement as we helped with the unloading. The tents, large bell-shaped khaki types, had already been erected by the men in a field.

We were quickly allocated tents. Mine, which I shared with five others from different packs, was at the end of the row and slightly on the slant, but it looked great. We soon unpacked, hung our mugs on a home-made mug tree and our outer clothes on large hooks embedded into the centre pole of the tent. We chose our bedding spot and laid down the ground sheet with the rolled up bedding and kitbag on top. We were not allowed to unroll the bedding until just before supper, by which time it would be just light enough to do the job before darkness came. The tent was inspected by the leader for neatness before we were ordered to go and prepare our first supper. Later, in the dusk by the camp fire, we sat in a circle singing silly songs, laughing and talking until the whistle went at 9pm for us to retire for the night. My first day camping had gone well and

I had thoroughly enjoyed it.

We awoke early next morning after only a few hours sleep. It had been too exciting a day and we had laid in our small beds chatting quietly for a long time. At 7am we dressed and put on our plimsolls. A short distance away were several washrooms. The outer walls of each consisted of sheets of canvas nailed to long poles hammered into the ground and tethered at the bottom with small tent pegs. The washrooms were three-sided with a loose canvas curtain we could pull to one side and let drop down behind us after entering. In the wind it gave no privacy whatsoever. The wash stand stood in the centre. It was a three-legged contraption, tied together with thick string, and wobbled all the time it was in use. On one of the branches, someone had placed a hook to hang the towel or a mug. Outside, just near to the curtain entrance, was a large bucket of cold water. When we had finished our ablutions, we had to carry our dirty water in the tiny basin to a large plastic dustbin-sized container at the end of the row so that we could dispose of it. Later the full container was taken away and emptied and returned for use next day. The most water the little basin held was about four inches, but at our age that was quite sufficient. All other toilet matters had to be completed back in the tent. One guide thought to take a mirror and we queued to use it to

Woodhouse Eaves (Leicester City Council)

make sure our hair was tidy or our beret was put on straight. We queued for everything: the washrooms, the latrines - of similar design to the washrooms and situated at the other end of the field - and of course, for meals.

Dressed in our uniforms and black plimsolls we set to making breakfast of sausages, fresh bread sent up from the village, and tea. This was followed by the washing up and tidying of our tents. Everything was inspected.

Our first day at camp was Sunday, and at 9am we were told to change our plimsolls for well-polished black lace-up shoes and parade for inspection. It was time for church parade. When our leader was satisfied that we all looked presentable, we were marched off in a column of twos into the village to attend the Sunday morning service.

For three days we threw ourselves into camp life and enjoyed every minute. A strict routine was established and we stuck rigidly to the duty rota for the chores. No one complained. Before leaving home, Mum had given me two pre-addressed and stamped postcards. All I had to do was write a few words on each, sign them and post them. I remember posting one and saying what a great time we were having, but I mislaid the other.

On the Wednesday it rained so hard that we had to eat our meals inside the large mess tent and sit around reading and playing games. It rained in torrents all day. At bedtime, the rain seemed to be a lot worse and we retired to bed early for warmth, and because we had nothing better to do. Reading by torchlight became a strain after a time. We lay in bed listening to the rain thundering on the tent roof. Worse was to come. Just after midnight we were woken by an enormous clap of thunder, followed by lightning. We lay there listening to it and watching the flashes of lightning through the thin canvas. We spoke quietly to one another trying to show that we were not afraid. Eventually, the dreadful noise faded away, the rain eased off to a drizzle and we fell asleep again.

At about 4.30am I awoke to the sound of running water very close to my head. I put out my hand to feel for the torch but felt only cold water. As I groped in the darkness, my hand became very wet and cold with slime. I shivered and located the torch. When I switched it on and flashed it around the tent floor, my bed looked as if it was floating. I shouted the others and by the light of their torches we saw that the whole of the tent was awash with water. It was running in one side and out the other. My ground sheet had protected the bedding but where the sheet and blanket had gone over onto the grass, it was soaking wet. I pulled on my wellingtons and a top coat and ran across to leader's tent to report we had been flooded out. She picked up a large torch and covered her night attire with a top coat. Her feet, she slid into a pair of sandals. When we approached our tent, all the girls were complaining of wet bedding and clothing. The leader stood and examined the bedding and slowly sank down into the ground. Her shoes were covered in mud and the water was soaking her feet. We were instructed to wait where we were, collect all our dry bedding and clothing, and to gather up any other personal belongings.

About half an hour later she returned, accompanied by an elderly gentleman she introduced as the Colonel. We were marched quickly through the darkness and drizzling rain across the field to the Colonel's property. We entered his extremely large house and were led to the great hall. There we were handed dry blankets and told to make ourselves comfortable on the highly polished wooden floor. We were to stay there for the remainder of the night. An elderly lady suddenly appeared carrying a tray of cups and mugs containing hot cocoa. While we drank it, she indicated the toilets, made sure we were comfortable and turned off some of the lights. When we had finished the cocoa, she collected the pots and left. Our leader made us promise to behave and not to touch anything. We had got so cold and damp that the warmth in the hall, dry blankets and hot cocoa knocked us out and we slept soundly.

The following morning we were allowed to have a lie in because of our disturbed night, and it was about 8.30am

Old John, Bradgate Park (Leicester City Council)

by the time we had dressed and been collected to return to the campsite for breakfast. We were ordered to leave everything tidy. Our nights under canvas had finished. We were to spend the rest of the week sleeping in the hall.

We returned to the field and as we approached saw that our tent was even more on the slope. It did not look safe. All around it was mud and great pools of water. It was a good job we were wearing wellingtons because we sank into the earth and mud with every step. Our tent was still flooded and actually stood in a shallow pool of water. We removed the remainder of our belongings. My bedding was soaked through. The dark green dye from the blanket had badly stained the sheet. We hung bedding and wet clothing on a clothes line rigged up between two tents and on the hedgerow at the side of the field. The sun came out, the temperature rose and the bedding began to steam from the heat of the sun. I was quite worried about my sheet and hoped my mother would not grumble about it. It was not my fault and I hoped she would understand.

For the rest of our stay that week, the weather was beautiful. Camp life went on as normal except at bedtime, when we were marched across to the hall to spend the night. During the day we went on long walks and orienteering expeditions, putting all our skills to good use.

The Friday turned out to be the hottest day and we all went to Bradgate Park for our last afternoon. We were allowed to wear civvy clothes, so we stripped down to the coolest of blouses and skirts. Several of us decided to walk along the path to Old John, but it was so hot we sat down a number of times on the grass mounds for a rest. There was one particular mound that struck extremely hot to the touch. We knelt down, running our hands all over it. Then we saw thin vapours of smoke or steam rising from various places. We decided that there was a fire underneath the ground. We ran to the car park, situated near Old John, to report our discovery to the park ranger. Exhausted and sweating, we hurried back with him to show him the exact spot and he verified that we had found the start of an underground fire. The combustion build up beneath would break through and cause a large fire. He staked out the area and ran back to call out the fire brigade. We stayed around to watch.

When the fire brigade arrived, they dug deep holes and let out the steaming air. Then they doused the area with water. We were complimented on our quick action and the fire brigade were able to avert a nasty bush fire. It did not seem possible that there could have been such fires in view of the extreme wet weather only a couple of days beforehand.

As time was getting on, we had to leave and get back to the troop assembling in the car park at the opposite end of the park. During the return to camp we all spoke at once, explaining what had happened, and our escapade became the talk of the camp.

The following morning we packed up and returned to Leicester. We were all sad and quiet during the ride back. Dad met me at the dispersal point and, after lots of goodbyes, we made our way home.

That night in the local newspaper there was an account of the incident at Bradgate Park, and it stated that a group of girl guides had adverted a large fire by their quick action. No names were given but we were proud to admit it was us.

That was my first and last experience of camping. There was never the opportunity to go again. We had lived on baked beans, sausages, fresh baked bread from the village shop, prunes and apples, fresh milk from the local farm, and tea. We all had colds and diarrhoea. We had been washed out, drenched and sunburnt but we had loved every minute.

Potato picking and paper rounds

When I was thirteen years old I realised the need for money. Not that I spent much, usually a couple of pence on a comic, a visit to the local cinema or saving to buy cards and birthday presents. As Christmas drew near and my circle of friends expanded, the small pocket money given to me each week was definitely not going to be sufficient. Also, there had been mention of a holiday the following year and I needed money towards that. So, with all this expenditure in mind, I set about job hunting. As if by magic the opportunity to earn money came quicker than I expected.

One day at school we were handed a circular from the local education committee explaining that children were needed to assist with the potato harvest. We had to take the circular home and if our parents agreed, they were to sign it and return it by the end of the week. The circular stated that the education department

and the farmers' union had made an arrangement, if parents consented, to employ children over the age of 12 years, working two days a week, on a Monday and Wednesday, or, Tuesday and Thursday, on the local farms potato picking. The working period would be in school hours, including travel, with two breaks and one hour for lunch. The children chosen for this work would receive three shillings a day. A perk of the job was to take home a small bag of free potatoes.

It all sounded exciting and I could not wait to get home and have my form signed. The idea of earning six shillings a week was a great temptation. Mother was not sure about it because she knew it would be hard work and thought it slave labour. I begged to go and eventually, after thinking about it for a couple of days and discussing it with Dad, she signed. The form, together with those of my friends, was handed in and we eagerly awaited the day the names of those chosen would be read out during assembly. There was no lack of volunteers and far more names were submitted than the quota for the school. Some children thought it would be great to miss schoolwork a couple of days a week but they were soon in for a shock. On the morning the names were read out before the whole school, I was among several of my friends chosen. We were told that the days we would be working and the names of the farms would be given to us on the Friday afternoon before finishing school. This was so that parents were aware of where we were and be able to arrange our packed lunches. We were instructed to take nothing valuable or money, just a cup. The farmer would provide hot tea. We were advised to wear old, but warm clothing as it was spring and invariably cold out in the fields. Every child was instructed to wear woollen socks and wellingtons. Those without were not allowed to go.

We had to be at the school gate by 8.40am to leave on the coach. On our arrival at the farm, we were shown to a large barn where we had to leave our lunch boxes and bags stacked in a corner. The toilet was indicated and we were advised to make use of it before going down to the field. No child was allowed to wander away from the working area. Escorted by the farmer or his labourer, we were led in crocodile file to the field to start work at 10am. Large hessian sacks were placed in piles at certain distances across the field. We had to stand clear as the tractor was driven slowly along a row of potatoes. When it was some distance away, we followed it. If we did not keep our distance, we soon discovered that mud, potatoes and stones, thrown up by the tractor, felt very hard when they rained down on top of us. We each held a sack and as we filled it with potatoes, began to drag it along the ground because of the increasing weight. When it became too heavy, we left it on the row and took another. We gradually filled numerous sacks by running backwards and forwards behind the tractor as it slowly wound its way up and down the field. The farmer, driving an open topped lorry, would make periodic visits along the rows, collecting the sacks and stacking them onto the lorry. To make sure we kept going and did not mess about, he would leave another pile of empty sacks for our use.

About 11.30am we stopped for a ten minute break, sitting on the half-filled sacks for a rest. We were glad of it. The work was much harder than we anticipated and we were kept at it all the time. We had to keep up with the tractor and clear a row before he made his return journey. About 12.30pm or 1pm, depending on the row to be completed, we were stopped for lunch and escorted back to the barn. There we collected our lunch packs and queued up with our cups and mugs for the steaming hot tea poured from an urn or large kettle by the farmer's wife. Sitting on the haystacks, we ate our sandwiches of jam or paste. It was at this time that I had my first taste of Marmite and cold toast with jam and cheese. We often shared our food and I had a friend who brought Marmite sandwiches one day and cold toast with jam and cheese the next. I sampled them in return for the odd egg or tomato sandwich and enjoyed the variety. We were allowed to play in the barn and had a great time sliding down the stacks and playing hide and seek. Sometimes, if time allowed, we were taken to see the cows or the chickens but always accompanied by someone attached to the farm. An hour later we were back at work. For the rest of the day we grovelled and scrapped about in the soil, collecting as many potatoes as possible. At 3.30pm we were allowed to collect our small bag of spuds and return to the coach and home.

Full of aches and pains, I proudly presented Mum with my bag of potatoes. She was very upset and annoyed when she saw the state I was in. She took the bag and contents and dropped it on the kitchen floor. I protested loudly.

'First things first,' she declared, 'Look at you. What a mess!' I had left the house clean and tidy and had returned filthy. The wellington boots were caked in mud. These Mum pulled off and flung into the yard. She immediately set about stripping me down and grumbling all the time that it was not worth all the trouble and mess. After a hot bath and some dinner, I fell asleep, worn out. Mother queried the wisdom of consenting to such a venture and tried to persuade me to give it up. I was stubborn and pleaded to continue. I intended to finish what I had started, come what may.

The potato picking lasted six weeks. The most outlying farm to be visited was in Lincolnshire, where we spent more time travelling than working. We became wise to the tea breaks and put the odd biscuit or bar of chocolate in our pocket to sustain us between breaks. We worked in the sunshine or the rain, in fields clogged with mud where our boots squelched and became as heavy as lead. We fought the March winds in the open fields and sweated beneath woollen clothes on warm spring days. The money was a great temptation to keep going. Dirt and soil were ingrained into our fingers and nails for weeks afterwards.

I handed over every penny I earned to Mother to save for me. She said that I ought to spend it on myself, as I had worked hard for it. She gave me a choice - something to wear or shoes. I chose a pair of summer sandals and saved the rest for a holiday.

My next venture in earning money was to take on a paper round. Our nearest newsagent, in St Saviour's Road, advertised for an early morning lad. I called in on my way home from school for details. I was kept waiting a good ten minutes while the newsagent discussed employing me. I was a female and usually the job went to the boys.

'OK, start tomorrow, seven sharp. Tell your parents the round takes about three-quarters of an hour.' And that was that. I had secured the job at the princely sum of seven shillings and sixpence a week. All I had to do was tell my parents.

Mum was not sure that I had done the right thing but she agreed to encourage me by getting me up at 6.45am the following morning. As I was never to go out first thing in the morning without something in my stomach, she made me tea and toast while I dressed. I was instructed that when I was used to the round, I would have to get up by myself and she found me an old alarm clock to use.

When I arrived at the shop, I discovered I was the only girl among ten boys. I took a lot of teasing from them. Fortunately, the newsagent's wife had written the name of each street on the top paper of those to be delivered as she had placed them into the large green canvas bag. Then she gave me a list of numbers. I had to work out who had what, sticking strictly to the order the papers came out of the bag from front to rear. The bag was extremely heavy. I stopped several times to rest it on the ground but I had to keep going to get done on time. I found the round was

large, starting in St Saviour's Road, then Asfordby Street, London Street, across Green Lane Road, Duxbury Road and all the streets on the left of Uppingham Road towards Spinney Hill Road. I kept the canvas bag because I went straight home on completing the round, but I had to make sure I remembered to take it with me again next morning. The newsagent was very strict and sacked any child who did not do the job properly. There were always plenty of other boys and girls ready to step into our shoes.

The first week was rather hectic trying to remember all the numbers and commit the round to memory. That first day took me a long time, well over an hour, and Mum became quite worried. Things quickly improved and I was able to cut down on my time by running and finishing the round in half an hour. At Christmas I was instructed to knock on the doors and say, 'Compliments of the season,' before handing over the paper. This was so I could reap the benefit of Christmas boxes to help my wages. I was pleasantly surprised to receive many good tips from satisfied customers.

One Saturday the newsagent asked me to consider doing a Sunday morning round. It would have to be covered twice, the first time delivering the paper and the second time collecting the money. I would start at 8am, be given a book with the names and addresses of the customers owing, and a float of two pounds in small change in a brown leather shoulder bag. In all, it should take one hour and a half. For this Sunday round I would receive five shillings. Easy, I thought and agreed.

On the Sunday morning I started feeling quite proud of the responsibility and the fact that I was trusted sufficiently to collect money and hand over the correct change. At 1pm, Mum was round at the newsagents demanding to know where I was. I was still out collecting. Being very conscientious, I had visited twice those addresses where they had failed to answer my knocking. I was determined to collect all the monies required. It had taken a lot of doing and I had taken much abuse. By 1pm I had a very heavy bag of money, felt extremely tired and had had enough. When I returned to the newsagents I was told to go straight home as Mum was looking for me. I had been out too long.

There was no thanks for the money collected. The five shillings wages were thrust into my hand. Mum was so cross when I arrived home she forbade me to do a Sunday round again. She kept insisting that it was the proprietor's job to have gone looking for me when he realised it was taking me a long time. Anything could have happened to me. In addition she said it was his job to collect money owing by customers not the delivery girls. When I thought about it I had to agree. I did not tell her of all the abuse and obscenities thrown out at me by some of the customers who objected to being woken up on a Sunday morning and being asked for money.

On the following Monday morning I enquired if the money had tallied with what was owed in the paying in book. The proprietor condescended to say that I had done well, especially getting payment from those customers who had not settled a paper bill for weeks! That Sunday round was my one and only despite the newsagent making further requests for me to do it again.

Later, when I was 15 and started to work, the paper round subsidised my small weekly wage. I managed to complete the round in time to clock in at work at 8am. At 16 things changed and I reluctantly gave up being a paper girl.

However, the job had satisfied me and helped with extra cash when I most needed it. I joined the Christmas Club at the newsagent's and paid a small sum out of my weekly wage towards gifts. I remember buying a lovely pale green water set for Mum. Over the years she broke all of the six

tumblers but the jug still remains. Then came the purchase of an artificial Christmas tree and some decorations - still in use today. One of my prized possessions and a constant reminder of those days, is a book, *Wuthering Heights*. It cost seven shillings and sixpence, purchased at sixpence per week. I recall seeing a powder compact in the chemist's shop on East Park Road and thinking what a beautiful Christmas gift it would be for Mum. It was two pounds and ten shillings, an enormous sum of money to me, but I joined the Christmas club and paid a little each week towards it. By Christmas Eve there was still a shilling to pay. I had to seek help from Dad and owe him. The compact was gold metal, with a bevelled edge and a flat oval centre, and had a black velvet bag to keep it in. Mum was thrilled to receive it and always kept it for best.

The majority of my paper earnings went towards holiday expenses or was saved through the Post Office Savings.

Mum's Christmas present (V. Tedder)

Of mice and man

'Oh not another,' cried Mother in desperation, pointing to a mouse as it flew across the kitchen floor.

'Well you knew we'd have some living next door to the dye works,' replied Dad, with raised eyebrows. 'Leave it to me. I'll get rid of them in a day or two.' And he did.

He found four small holes in the skirting boards. One in the front room, two in the living room and another in the kitchen near to the coal store. His system was easy and successful. He baited the traps with bacon and cheese, then left them unset outside the holes. Overnight the mice visited, found the food, removed it and disappeared. The next evening, Dad baited the traps with similar food but set them properly. It always worked and it was a quick death for the mice.

It was no good being afraid of them and we knew there would always be some able to find their way into the house. It was obvious that mice would be attracted to the bales of wool and parcels of paper stored in the factory. Often, when Dad helped the workers remove bales and paper, they came across nests of baby mice, snug and comfortable in the warmth of the factory. I saw several lots, all pink and rubbery looking. Also there was always plenty to eat in the factory. The workers were very careless with their lunch boxes and sandwich wrappers, daily leaving a variety of scraps for the mice to find and enjoy.

The mice seemed to come into our house in batches of three or four a week and always when the workers were having a shift around with the stored bales. We became used to seeing a little body disappearing around the back of the sideboard or the gas cooker in the kitchen. They always ran when the electric lights were switched on.

Our floors were covered with linoleum and rugs. As the living room consisted of two rooms knocked into one,

there was a long corridor mat laid down the centre. Often when we had been out for the evening and switched on the light on our return, we would see one or two mice running down the centre of the long rug and skid on the highly polished floor in their panic. They would travel so fast that their legs would be running on the spot as they slipped and slithered towards the door or the skirting board, and frequently they crashed against the wall unable to stop themselves in time. Sometimes if we were sitting quietly reading or sewing we could hear the plop plop as one hopped down one step to another on the stairs. It was quite amusing to watch them running at breakneck speed in their fright and haste to get away to a safe hole.

Mum and Dad were very vigilant and did everything possible to discourage them and get rid of them. Mother was extremely fastidious and covered all food and kept it in tightly closed cupboards.

Our biggest headache, and the most horrendous matter we had to deal with, was the sudden arrival of cockroaches. We had seen several batches over the first year or two and they were disposed of as quickly as they arrived. These too we began to accept as part of the living conditions, although we hated the creepy things. However, we were not prepared for the onslaught that met us one evening when we returned home after dark.

We entered the gateway from the street and our path to the back door was lit by the light from the Jackson's living room. Mum opened the back door and switched on the kitchen light. She was always able to keep fairly calm about the mice but on this night she let out a shriek. When we looked to where she was pointing, we saw that the kitchen was alive with dozens and dozens of cockroaches. The kitchen was white-washed and they showed up easily against the walls. Mother shouted her disgust and shuddered. In fact, she swore. We made so much commotion, the Jacksons came out and Mum asked them to take Julie into their home while we coped with getting rid of the cockroaches. Mother said that this was the last straw and we were going to move house.

When Mum switched on the light, the cockroaches ran everywhere in their effort to get out of the light. Poor Dad. He grabbed a tea towel in one hand and with his other bare hand, began scooping them up. He turned on the water tap in the sink and swished many down the plughole. The sound of others he cracked underfoot still remains with me today. I thought it the most horrible sight I had ever seen. Screwing up my nose and flinching, I helped them to get rid of as many as possible before they disappeared into all the dark corners. It seemed ages before we were satisfied. We pulled out furniture, pots and pans, and anything that had a dark corner for them to hide in. Eventually, we were satisfied that we could sleep safely in our beds. Upstairs. We had not thought of that. Carefully, I followed my parents as they went through the house, up the stairs and into the bedrooms. Nothing. For some reason, they had not ventured beyond the kitchen and the adjacent living room. From then on, each time we returned home after dark we dreaded what we would find. There were always a few but never as many as we found on that particular night.

The dye works closed down each year for two weeks at the time of the August bank holiday period. It took this length of time to have the machinery overhauled and repaired, and for the factory to have a general spring clean. Some painting always needed to be done and the large dye and salt vats were cleaned and sterilised.

The boilers closed down completely for the first week, needing servicing, cleaning and invariably, repairs. However, before repairs could be undertaken and any new parts fitted, Dad and George Thorpe had the unpleasant job of cleaning them out. It was a filthy chore and took several days to complete. Sometimes the boilers needed attention from outside engineers and Dad was always on hand to assist. Frequently, he was able to do running repairs himself. After 18 years in the navy, there was not much about

boilers that he did not know. Unfortunately, the boss was not so knowledgeable and often refused replacements, telling Dad to repair the job as well as he could. Consequently, this led to some severe breakdowns and the factory would come to a sudden halt until a new part was acquired and fitted. Dad pointed out that the 'make do and mend' attitude of the boss was uneconomical, causing far more expense and inconvenience.

The boiler, as far as I remember, was a great black and brown cylindrical contrivance with two inner boilers that ran side by side for the full length of the boiler house. The large iron doors became red hot and had to be opened and closed by using the edge of the coal shovel. A latch was lifted and the doors swung back easily on the well greased hinges. Above the doors were two large coal hoppers that fed the coal into the boilers a little at a time. Dad had the job of filling them with coal and pressing a button to haul the hoppers up and back into place. All across the front of the boilers were numerous gauges and brass pipes. One gauge, prominently fixed at the front, had half the face in red. Dad often stated that if the boiler became overheated and dangerous, the needle would pass across to the red zone. If that happened, he switched everything off and retreated. It was his job to make sure the gauge remained in the neutral position. I was always fascinated by the gauges as they flicked from side to side. The heat in the boiler house had to be felt to be believed. I never knew how he managed to work under such conditions but I guess he was used to it.

I believe we had been living in the house for about three years when Dad decided he had had enough of working long hours at the factory for a very small wage of three pounds per week. One day, he was furious when he discovered that the dyers were taking home between fifteen to eighteen pounds a week. He felt he was not receiving the correct wage for all his knowledge and experience. The factory could not function without him maintaining and coaxing the boilers into action. He was up early every morning, lighting and fuelling the boilers to get up steam for the hot water used in the dye works. In the evenings he had to tend the boilers and shut them down safely overnight. Saturdays and Sundays the boilers still required attention, and he was constantly cleaning and servicing the machinery because it was getting very old. So, quite rightly, he went to see the boss, Mr John Wilson, and asked for a rise in wages. I do not know what happened but Dad came home very upset and said that he was going to resign and look for another job. Later, he told us that his request was flatly refused and, after an argument, Dad gave notice to leave at the end of the week.

Mum was rather upset and extremely worried in case he was not able to find suitable work. However, he was lucky and obtained employment at the Standard Engineering Company on Evington Valley Road. He was offered work at three pounds ten shillings a week, regular hours of 8am to 5pm and weekends off - a great improvement. My parents appeared much happier than they had been for a long time. George Thorpe, who had assisted Dad with the boilers, was given the job of boilerman permanently and some weeks later Dad discovered he had been given a rise of ten shillings!

From then on, although Dad felt more secure financially, the conditions at the house seemed to get worse. Mum made enquiries at the Leicester City Housing Department for a council house, but apart from having our names added to the list, because our house was sturdy and roomy she was told that we were unlikely to be given a council house. Mum even tried to get us re-housed by consulting the doctor and complaining that our living conditions were a health risk, but he told her that because we did not suffer any long term illnesses as a result of the conditions, there was nothing he could do to help us. So, life went on among the smells, dirt and dust as usual.

Then came the time when the boss called to see us one afternoon and requested permission to store a few large bales containing parcels of unbleached wool, in the gateway. In addition to giving access to the gate belonging to the factory, the gateway was our right of way. We had to agree over matters concerning anything that might obstruct access. Mother was instantly suspicious, stating it was the beginning of them storing anything to do with dye works in the gateway and another method of trying to drive us out of the house.

It was well known at that time that the boss wanted to extend his offices by knocking through the wall in our front room. With all this in mind, Mother hesitated in giving consent. The boss explained that they had secured a very large order but unfortunately, all the wool to be dyed had to be delivered to the factory at the same time. There was insufficient room to store the bales in the factory and he just wanted to put the extra ones in the gateway until required for dyeing. He said that the workers would be instructed to start on the bales in the gateway first and that he estimated they would all be removed within a couple of weeks.

Well, it was agreed that as long as there was a good passage down the yard and access to the front and back doors of both houses, he could store the bales for that short time. Mother was dubious and kept repeating that we should be sorry for giving consent. But what could we do? In a way we had to keep in with the wishes of the boss to a certain extent to keep a roof over our heads, but we all felt we had made a wrong move.

Within a couple of days a great lorry arrived outside the house. It was so long and high that it dwarfed the five houses and blocked the street for a couple of hours while the bales were unloaded. The factory workers pulled together and, using trolleys, ran in and out of the factory unloading the enormous bales. Then it came to our turn. We watched as the men gradually filled the gateway leaving just about eighteen inches between the bales to get down to the back doors. They were piled one on top of another and I was always in fear of the top ones tipping and falling on top of us and injuring us. They were so heavy, packed tight with parcels of wool and the hessian sacks stretched tightly round them and held in place with thin rope.

Within a few days of being stored, the cockroaches were back. This time they confined themselves to the yard but it was nothing to fetch a few items of washing in from the line and see a couple clinging on. At night, Dad would go out with a torch, finding and killing as many as he could in order to keep them out of the house. Mum stopped opening her windows and we blocked up the bottom of the front door with a snake shaped cushion. Many found their way into the kitchen, attracted by the warmth, but they did not last long when Dad did his rounds. Anyway, in order to keep control, my parents kept a nightly patrol until all the bales were removed. It was several months before the bales were taken into the factory. They were not the first to be used as promised. There were many occasions after that when the boss requested bales be stored in our gateway and having given consent once, he could not be refused. Eventually, he stopped asking permission and stored them when and as often as he liked. Many a time we went out for the day and, on opening the wicket gate on our return, found we had to pick our way between piles of bales to get to the back door. The Jacksons next door never objected once and never backed my parents when they made their complaints about the litter, strings, tags and old wool that was left lying about the yard. Sometimes we would see Mrs Jackson hurry out of her back door with the sweeping brush and a carrier bag. Quickly she would sweep up the bits and pieces, put them into her dustbin and hurry back in home again. We felt sure she did not want us to know she was clearing up the mess left by the workers, because she did not want to be involved in any arguments.

There were times when the whole bale was not removed and the dyers in their hurry, would tear open the bags, lift out the specified number of parcels they required and leave the paper, string and tags on the ground. Mum was always following them around, picking up what they had dropped. She felt she had to do it for our benefit as there was a limit to how many times she could go to the boss and complain. Again, it became a way of life and we grew to accept it.

Friends and neighbours

There were many periods when my parents went through difficulties which ended in shouting matches and arguments. Dad seemed to take a long time to settle after the war and being at sea for 18 years in the Royal Navy. He suffered, as many others did, from the traumatic experiences of battle which left him mentally scarred for life.

Mother, having gained her independence by working full time during the war, had gone through the stage where

The Rifle Butts public house (Mr J. Zientek)

Julie and Bernard Crossley at Wicksteed Park (V. Tedder)

I was off her hands to a certain extent. Then she found herself pregnant with my sister and that, together with the move to Nottingham Road, tested her patience. She was very fastidious and the conditions brought about by the dye works infuriated and sickened her. She was not at all happy with the restrictions that having a new-born child brought and felt trapped. Dad felt he was boxed in and, with such small wages, unable to improve our lot. Altogether this led to a great strain on our domestic life and the slightest thing seemed to start them off arguing. It was extremely distressing to me to hear my adored parents acting in this manner. Frequently, I would put my sister in her pram and go for long walks around the streets or take her onto Spinney Hill Park, hoping that by the time we returned home the rows would be over.

The funny part about the arguing was that after a

shouting match of several minutes, Mother would put her finger to her lips and shush Dad, saying that she didn't want the neighbours to hear them. Dad was a pacifist and it took a lot to get him going but there were times when he threatened to strangle Mum if she didn't stop nagging. They usually made it up and we girls were never included in the rows.

Our neighbours were nosy and missed nothing. We were watched in and out of the house from behind lace curtains. The elderly lady across the road, opposite, was the worst. We could not move without her watching us from behind drawn curtains. We used to laugh about it but Mother became rather annoyed.

One day, Mrs Jackson told us a story about the elderly lady, Mrs Jeffs, which made us laugh and Mum ease off moaning about her. The five houses opposite were terraced with front doors that opened onto the street. Access to the rear was gained by walking past the front door, turning left into Lancaster Street and a short walk past the corner shop and their garden, to turn left again into an open alleyway. Each house had a small garden and a back gate that opened onto the alley.

The story, and we have no reason not to believe it was true, concerned Mrs Jeffs who was married to a man who liked his pint of beer. Several in fact, and he was often seen coming home drunk. It was his habit to visit The Rifle Butts public house in Nottingham Road and stagger home after closing time. He usually made his way to the rear of the house, via the alleyway. However, on one particular evening in summer he was late coming home and his wife watched for him from behind closed lace curtains in the front room. As he approached the front door which was slightly ajar, a hand shot out grabbing him by the scruff of the neck and he was yanked up the steps and into the house as quick as a flash. The door closed with a bang. Mrs Jeffs would never admit her husband was a drunk but she was seen to haul him in through the front door in this manner on numerous occasions.

The rest of the neighbours opposite were pleasant, but went about their business and kept themselves to themselves. They were of the modern era and were not prone to neighbouring like the old folks.

In the next gateway was old Mrs Turville's house, and opposite lived the Crossleys, Oliver and May and their son Bernard. They had their living room and kitchen screened off by a six foot fence and gate. This gave them a private yard away from the prying eyes of the factory workers. Their gateway led straight down to the boiler room and the stacks of coal, and was wider than ours, giving more room for the lorries to reverse when making their deliveries. Apart from the coal-dust and the factory smells, the Crossleys did not have as much to put up with from the factory as we did.

As Julie and Bernard became older they played together most days either in our home and yard or his. Bernard enjoyed playing with dolls and teacups and Julie enjoyed his building bricks and motor cars. They were good friends and were not prone to squabbling over the toys. When they reached their teens and found other friends and interests they still managed to remain friends, although they drifted apart. When the Crossleys purchased a property in Fleckney and moved house, we visited them occasionally but eventually lost touch with them.

On the corner of Nottingham Road and Lancaster Street was a shop. It had been several establishments over the years but we knew it when it was a cobblers for a time. Then the property was sold and became a family home.

A grocery shop occupied the corner of Nottingham Road and Rosebery Street. It was the family business of Bodicoat and Sons. Although the shop appeared quite small, the whole of the premises took up a large part of the corner. Mother went to this shop for all her groceries. I remember seeing lard and butter, weighed and cut to size from great slabs, patted into shape before being wrapped in greaseproof paper. Coffee and loose tea were weighed into various coloured bags. The coffee grinding machine was painted red and stood high on the end of the counter near the shop entrance. The smell was gorgeous. There were bacon and ham which were placed onto a white enamel machine with a large handle which was turned by hand as the meat or bacon was sliced to the customer's requirements. A small chart indicated the thickness the meat could be sliced, from size one to nine. It was a very happy, efficiently run, family business and nothing was too much trouble. Roy Bodicoat, the son, was in the navy during the war and he and Dad became good friends. There were several helping in the shop over a period of time, but as a teenager I was not too observant or bothered. I do recall that Roy's wife, Wooky, who was a Wren during the war, also helped in the shop and became a friend to Mum.

At the bottom of Nottingham Road, at the junction with East Park Road, stood Les Randall's butchers shop. This too was a family run concern. Mr Randall was very obliging and his mother, despite her good age, helped in the shop when he was busy. I was fascinated on Saturday mornings when I went for the weekend joint, watching him cutting the meat to just the exact weight the customer requested. There was never, 'It's a little bit over,' or 'Sorry, it's a little bit under.'

He had a speciality that was a favourite with the local constabulary - the early morning fry-up. It consisted of bacon, sausage, a lamb chop, two whole kidneys and a piece of liver. Many a police officer called to collect his parcel of fry-up en-route to the police station at Asfordby Street or Uppingham Road when it was time for a meal break.

Just around the corner on East Park Road, and situated opposite the Imperial Typewriter factory, the first launderette in the area opened. Mother eyed it with suspicion at first thinking of the cost, until she realised it was ideal for drying the great grey army blanket curtain. When she discovered how successful it was she followed it by washing all the bed blankets and drying them in the large drying machines.

I remember one evening after a row with Dad she put a small pile of washing into a bag, picked Julie up in her arms and, ordering me to follow her, left the house and marched down to the launderette where we sat watching the clothing going through a full wash cycle. Mum said that we would return home when Dad had cooled down. However, we stayed too long because the drying machine went wrong and would not stop. By the time the engineer had arrived and stopped the machine and we arrived home, Dad was worried sick about us being out so late.

He told Mum she had been very silly and as stubborn as ever. Mother retaliated and started off another argument. Julie was put to bed and I quickly followed. Eventually I heard Mum slam the living room door and come up to bed. Next day there was nothing to indicate they had been arguing. They were back to being friends again. Mum was always dubious about that certain drying machine and avoided using it.

Next to the launderette was a double fronted shoe shop. I bought several pairs of shoes from there because the prices always seemed a little cheaper than those in the city. Also it was possible to pay so much a week into a

Charnwood Street (Leicester City Council)

shoe club. I remember buying two pairs of shoes in this manner when I first started work. There was one stipulation - the shoes were retained by the shop until two thirds of the price had been paid in advance. I made sure that I started payment well in advance of the time I needed to wear the shoes. It was a hard way to acquire a pair of shoes and consequently, they were always treated with respect, cleaned and repaired and they lasted for years.

Then there was Charnwood Street, a road with every type of shop you could imagine from one end to the other. Frequently on a lovely sunny Sunday morning, we would go for a walk along the street from Spinney Hill Road to Nedham Street, fascinated by the little shops and the wares for sale. The shops closed at 1pm and all the crowds dispersed. Second-hand clothes and furniture shops were busy places. Second-hand jewellers and knick-knack shops held our attention. There was always something to catch the eye. I recall that Mum purchased several pairs of shoes from a discount store and lots of baby clothes for Julie. Fruit and vegetable, sweet and newsagents, cornershop grocers, all did a roaring trade between 8am and 1pm. If you could not get what you wanted in town, you usually could from one of the shops in Charnwood Street.

I had a relative named Wright who owned a small music shop along the street. He played accordion, sold pianos, sheet music and musical instruments. Years later when Charnwood Street began to lose its shops and folk moved away, he sold his shop and took up teaching the accordion at one of the large houses on University Road, which he converted into a music studio.

When Charnwood Street was pulled down to make way for better housing, the old community spirit and simple and honest trading for the less fortunate members of society was lost forever. Many remember Charnwood Street with affection.

Evington Road, 1940s. (Leicester City Museums)

CHAPTER THREE
Second chance

In the spring of 1947, I was given the opportunity to sit an examination for the entrance to an art and craft school. It was the equivalent to Gateway Boys School situated in the city and the maroon uniform was similar. I did not know much about it at the time but the fact that it seemed a good way out of Bridge Road School was appealing and sufficient to make me really concentrate on my lessons with a keenness to do well in the tests.

Part of the test was to produce to an examiner, during an interview, any items of art and craft that had been made or designed during the previous twelve months. Without a word to my parents, I sorted out a terry towelling teddy bear, a tortoise made from brown felt and highly embroidered with shell markings in yellow silk, several embroidered cushion covers and table runners which I hoped my mother would not miss from the sideboard, and a couple of handmade aprons and handkerchiefs. Not all of them had been made during the previous twelve months but I was eager to please and they had all been made by my own fair hand, albeit under the guidance of Mum during the long winter evenings. How could I be refused a place at the school with all this skill at my fingertips?

The written examination was difficult but I persevered with each paper. When it came to the interview, the elderly lady who saw me in the assembly hall carefully inspected each item I produced, writing notes on a paper attached to a clip board. Then came the waiting period.

A few weeks later, to my joy and my parents' frustration, an official notification was received to the effect that I had passed the examination and had been accepted for a place at the new Art and Craft School on Wigston Lane, Leicester. Term was to start in September and a list

Valerie, 1949 (V. Tedder)

of the uniform required was attached. Well, Mother nearly went mad. She was angry because she was unaware of the fact that I had sat the examination in the first place without telling her, and she chastised me with strong words including the fact that it was going to cost a lot of money. Anyway, I explained that it was just what I wanted and I would be far happier at the new school. She had to admit that my present one was not helping my progress. Anyway, after sleeping on it and talking it over with Dad, it was agreed that I could go. I was so excited about having another chance at a better school, it was like starting a new life.

Spinney Hill Park and East Park Road in the late 1940s. (Leicester City Museums)

The uniform caused a bit of a problem because cash was short, but Mum set about seeing what she could manage. Eventually, after weeks of searching the local paper and advertisements in the newsagent's shop window, she purchased two nearly new blouses from a woman who lived in Lancaster Street. The uniform skirt and school beret, both in a maroon colour, she had to purchase from the special school uniform shop in the city. She refused to buy a blazer when she saw the price and insisted she would knit me a cardigan in time for the commencement of school. This would tide me over until there were sufficient funds to purchase a blazer. However, that occasion never arose and I wore a beautifully hand-knitted cardigan until I left school, two years later.

Another expense was the gym slip. It was an all girls school and the gym mistress wanted to break away from the traditional navy knickers or shorts and a white vest.

She chose a blue rayon sleeveless dress with a short flared skirt. Two were required but Mum only purchased one from the school, on the weekly. Consequently it was forever being washed and ironed and eventually became much paler in colour and I knew some of the girls were aware of the reason. It lasted well, with the seams just beginning to fray when I finished school.

I enjoyed the Art and Craft School immensely and they were the happiest two years of my school life. It meant leaving home very early in the morning to arrive at school for 8.45am. I took the tram from East Park Road to F.W. Woolworth and Company Limited in Gallowtree Gate, then raced along Horsefair Street to catch a Corporation bus from Bowling Green Street to the school gates on Wigston Lane. Sometimes the journey home took longer when I decided to waste my threepenny tram fare on an ice cream from a stall in the market, or browse around the shops. It was all looking, there was no money to spend. On these occasions I had to walk home from the city. It was a long walk but, taken briskly, I could do it in about half an hour. I was not too late in arriving home, not so much that Mum noticed. The way was straight. Up and over Swain Street bridge, around the back of Hillcrest Hospital, through the streets to Melbourne Road, along Dale Street and across Spinney Hill Park. It was well worth the treat to myself. I recall I did this walk numerous times during the two years I attended the school and not once did I have any bother with men or youths approaching me or stopping me for anything. I always felt safe.

Lunch was taken, not on the school premises but at the Community Centre on Southfields Drive. We would walk along in crocodile file, accompanied by a couple of teachers. It took about twenty minutes but after lunch we were on our honour to behave and return under our own steam. If we ate our dinner quickly we had plenty of time to dawdle and be back just in time for the afternoon lessons. The dinners were good and plentiful and I do not remember many complaints. Frequently I would hurry my meal or miss a course so that I could visit the library on Southfields Drive. It was situated on the junction with Saffron Lane and Stonesby Avenue and known as the 'Pork Pie Library' because of its shape. I spent many hurried minutes choosing thriller books, and managed to read at least two a week while travelling on the public transport.

As soon as I started at the school one of the first lessons we attended was the sewing class. We were instructed that during the winter months we would be fully occupied making our uniform summer dresses for the following year. What a headache it became, especially to those in the classes that were good at everything else in the art line except sewing. I could sew reasonably well and managed to progress without a lot of supervision. However, we had to queue for the use of a sewing machine so I sought the help of Mum, and together we managed to finish my garments in time. The design was

intricate and the making up even worse. It was a style chosen to teach us the basic method of dressmaking and to cover a great many parts of the actual stitching. The style was complicated, having the material gathered onto yokes, back and front, and the gathering of the bodice and skirt into a waistband. Even the sleeves were gathered around the top and into a band at the bottom. Each band and the yokes had to be edged with white piping. Lastly, buttons and handmade buttonholes were sewn all the way down the front. It was a mammoth task and some of the girls who were rather slow had to stay behind on numerous days after school to get them finished in time for the summer term. The material chosen was green, white and maroon gingham. There were different sorts of checks to suit our individual taste but we had to have two dresses of the same material to be economical.

However, the dresses were very serviceable and washed well. I even managed to wear mine for work during the summer I left school, until I was able to earn enough money to buy material to make one or two dresses in styles more becoming a working girl.

Situated next door to the school was the Woodlands Remand Home for Boys. It was strictly out of bounds with the threat of instant expulsion if caught anywhere near. Their establishment was separated from the school grounds by a six foot high wooden slatted fence with a single strand of barbed wire across the top. However, curiosity got the better of us one day and three of us risked a quick run through the small wooded area on our side of the fence to take a look. We saw several boys of our age working in the grounds or on the gardens, with an adult male supervising them. It was exciting and thrilling but we were scared to death when one of the lads saw us and yelled out. We raced back to school entering by a rear door so we would not be discovered. We only went to look. There was no way we would approach the boys or hold a conversation with them.

I recall that one day, a couple of girls were caught red-handed by one of the teachers. They were silly enough to wave and call to the boys which had attracted her attention. They were marched quickly to the Headmistress to explain themselves. The following morning during assembly we were subjected to a lecture from the Headmistress. The boys were branded as wicked thieves, house breakers and robbers and for any of us to associate with them in any way was just as wicked. We were told that they were there as a punishment and it was extremely serious if the girls spoke to them. It was inviting instant dismissal. However the girls concerned were not expelled, but we were so scared that nobody ventured anywhere near the adjoining fence if they could avoid it.

The classes were split into two and given letters of the alphabet. I was in part E of EF and we were periodically given projects to complete. They varied in subjects but I was surprised when our half of the class were given gardens which we could cultivate as we wished. There were about eight gardens measuring roughly six feet square. There was sufficient room to grow small vegetables, salad produce or flowers. I chose the salad items. We were shown how to prepare the soil and set our seeds. In addition to the set lesson period we were expected to care for the garden in our own time, and at the end of the season or when the produce or flowers were ready to harvest, the teacher would inspect our work and mark us on our effort. We could take home anything we had grown. In my small patch I set spring onions, radishes, lettuce, carrots and beetroot. I was very successful and proud of my produce as it grew. The soil, having been well tended before we had it, was beautifully fine and rich with compost. Growing things was easy. I informed the teacher when my produce was about ready to be picked and arranged for her to check it and mark me on my efforts.

When I arrived with the teacher, I was horrified to see large gaps in the rows of spring onions and radishes. One or two of the lettuces were missing. Someone had helped themselves to my produce, and I was near to tears as I

explained they had been stolen and not removed by me in my keenness to try them out. Fortunately for me the teacher had kept abreast of the progress of the gardens and after a quick picking, smelling, examining and tasting a small portion from each of the salad items, she stated that I had done very well and gave me good marks. However, the gaps in the rows had spoilt the display and I was very upset. I was given permission to remove the remainder of the produce after school before it all disappeared. When I returned to gather the remains after school that afternoon, I actually caught a girl red-handed. She was pulling radishes from the garden, wiping the dirt off with her fingers and eating them there and then. I was so annoyed I rushed at her and pushed her to the ground. She choked on her titbit and I was delighted. She coughed until she made herself sick. 'Good punishment,' I shouted, as I quickly cleared the ground and took everything home. My dad was very pleased with the result.

One of the things I disliked about school was the sports arrangements. Firstly, we all had to have our own hockey stick and secondly, for the summer months, a tennis racquet and four balls.

Hockey I was not keen on but I was prepared to give it a try. I never felt the urge to go charging around a large field being bashed on the shins and ankles. Mother, unable to afford a new hockey stick, made her enquiries and ended up purchasing a second-hand one for me. Dad inspected it and rewrapped the cord binding around the handle where it was coming adrift. He made a good job of it and after cleaning and polishing, it looked in a better state than I had anticipated. When it came to sports day, the mistress in charge noted the names of all those with previous hockey experience and formed a team. The rest, including myself, were told to go onto the next hockey pitch and practice the moves she had spent about ten minutes explaining. From then on, it seemed that every sports day the chosen few were schooled in correct hockey procedure and eventually from this group she chose a number to play for the school. As for the rest of us it was practice, practice and practice. I remember racing around the field on numerous occasions trying to keep warm when the weather was cold and frosty. Full of hope that one day the teacher might need a substitute or a reserve team, I ran myself into the ground on occasions, trying to please her with all the right moves. But she had her eye on the initiated and we were rather slow to see that, as far as the newcomers and beginners were concerned, her interest was all pretence.

In the meantime, having suffered several agonising bangs on the shins and ankles, the teacher recommended shin-pads. Another expense I thought, but I needed protection. When bruise began to pile on top of bruise, I realised something had to be done and I approached my dad to purchase shin pads. This time it was he who refused. 'Put newspaper down the front of your sock,' he told me, 'The footballers do and the same can be done for hockey players'.

So, with no likelihood of being the possessor of strong, comforting shin-pads, I took his advice. When the next sports day came around, I went to school armed with two *John Bull* magazines. I folded them, bent them and pressed them against my legs to fit snugly. They felt very awkward. The paper was held in place under the socks with thin white elastic underneath the turn-over at the top and around the ankles. It did the trick and I was braver in my attack on the field. However, it was all in vain, as the

(V. Tedder)

CITY OF LEICESTER EDUCATION COMMITTEE

LEICESTER COLLEGE OF ART
ART SECONDARY SCHOOL FOR GIRLS

REPORT ON _Valerie Gisborn_, FORM _2ef_ FOR _Summer_ TERM, 194_9_

NUMBER IN FORM _23_ TERM POSITION _1_ EXAM. POSITION _2_ HONOURS _8_

TIMES ABSENT _14_ TIMES LATE _—_ SIGNATURES _—_

SUBJECT	TERM SECTION	EXAM. SECTION	REMARKS	STAFF
ARITHMETIC	2	5	Usually fairly careful and accurate. Examination very disappointing.	Des.
BIOLOGY ELEMENTARY SCIENCE	2	3.	Works well in class and has made improved.	Des.
ENGLISH LANGUAGE ENGLISH LITERATURE	3	2	Has worked very sensibly and well.	M.7.P.
GARDENING				
GEOGRAPHY	2	3	Good. Valerie has worked well think	REE
HISTORY	2	2.	A very sound terms work.	M.7.P.
INDIVIDUAL RESEARCH WORK	1	—	Very good work done.	N.B.
PHYSICAL TRAINING	1	—	Very good; is keen + works well.	N.B.
SCRIPTURE	3		Fairly good.	R.E.E.
BOOKCRAFTS				

49

teacher was not interested and I agreed it was not worth the expense. So, for two years at school, practice was the extent of my hockey playing.

Next came tennis. This was a bit different. I had always wanted to play tennis and thought that being keen, at last I would receive tuition and get somewhere. Again, my parents could not afford the purchase of a new racquet and balls, so a second-hand one was acquired. The racquet was in excellent condition and I looked forward to a summer of learning tennis. How wrong I was. The sports mistress lined us up on the tennis court and asked us who could play. Several stepped forward and she took them to the adjoining courts. We were given the balls and spent the majority of the lesson knocking them to and fro across the net. Over the next few weeks, she would leave us to have a knock-about while she gave tuition to a select few. From those she selected a couple to represent the school. We organised games among ourselves while she was away tutoring her favourites, but if she returned and found anyone standing about or in the middle of a game, she stopped it to give us a demonstration on how to serve or handle the racquet. She then left us standing in a line across the court practising what she had just demonstrated. And that was the extent of my tennis career. I never learned the game properly, and eventually lost interest.

We often discussed the way the teacher acted unfairly with us, and some of the girls who were not interested in any sport refused to back us when we tried to get up a deputation among those more articulate to complain to the Headmistress. It all seemed a waste of time, so we put up with our silly useless sports days, sending the chosen ones to Coventry, and played about behind the sports mistress's back. The funny thing was when the school reports were endorsed at the end of term, she always worded mine favourably and indicated my keenness and aptitude for sport. Where she got that from, I never knew.

Freewheeling

I had not been at the new school very long when Mother received notification that I was to attend the Clarendon Park Children's Clinic for an operation for the removal of my tonsils. There had been so many occasions of me suffering from throat infections that the doctor decided it was time for the operation and sent in a request for it to be performed as soon as possible in view of my age. However, it was such a long time coming that we had completely forgotten about it. I was 14 years of age and by all accounts rather old for that type of operation.

The letter indicated that I would be in hospital for two days but was required to inform the school that I would be absent for a week. Mother signed the form giving her consent for me to have the operation and returned it. The day arrived and, carrying a small holdall containing the items of clothing I needed, Mother and I travelled to the clinic by bus. We found that the hospital was a one storey establishment at the corner of Clarendon Park Road and London Road. It was surrounded by neat lawns and flower beds.

When we entered the building there was a distinct smell of disinfectant and everywhere was clinically clean. It was 10am when the doctor called us into his consulting room for a quick examination. Mother was asked numerous questions about my health and heart. I was declared free from infection and escorted to a small ward containing six beds. Mum left me after I was undressed and settled in bed. The ward slowly filled up with other children all under the age of nine years. I felt quite adult among them.

I remember having a light lunch that day but nothing else. I amused myself by either reading to myself or to the other children. At about 8pm we were bedded down for the night and given tablets with water. The operations were scheduled to commence early next morning.

We were awakened at about 6am by the ward sister who told us all to put on white woollen bed socks. We were then tucked up tightly in the sheets, soon to be overcome with drowsiness as the result of an injection we were given in the back of one of our hands. I lay and watched each child being carried out of the ward by a male porter. A short time afterwards the child was brought back by the porter, put into bed and the curtains drawn around it. I dozed in between each child being removed and returned. About 8.30am it was my turn.

Now I realised why I had not been put to sleep like the other children. I was too big to be carried, I had to walk to the theatre. With the porter on one side and the nurse on the other, I was supported in the short walk to the operating theatre. I shall never forget the sight that met me. In my drowsiness, I recall seeing a gleaming white room with great spotlamps hanging closely together over a long table draped with a white sheet and a rubber covering. Too big and heavy to be lifted onto the table, I was told to jump up and sit on it and then to swing my legs up and to lie down. I was very frightened as a sheet was placed over me. I felt my heart thumping away and I was trembling. Next a pear-shaped mask was placed over my mouth and nose and I began to panic a little, but the nurse holding the anaesthetic mask began to tell me a story about three little ducks swimming on a pond and I remembered nothing more. When I came round I was back in bed and the operation completed.

My throat was burning and extremely sore. I slept well into the afternoon and then woke up sufficiently to take sips of iced water. By the time evening came I was wide awake but unable to talk. The first night was awful. The other children constantly whimpered and were distraught wanting their mothers. The nurses were very good and comforted them back to sleep. The following morning we were encouraged to drink as much cold water or juice as possible and we ate mushy food. In the afternoon we were given a treat of ice cream. Mum came to visit me in the evening and arranged to take me home the next day. By this time, although my throat hurt, I was in and out of bed most of the time playing with the children and trying to keep them amused by drawing pictures and painfully reading fairy stories.

The following morning Mum arrived at 10am as instructed, but we had to wait until about 11.30am so that the surgeon could examine me before being discharged. We went home in a taxi, it was a real luxury. I looked forward to my week off from school and had made plans to go out as soon as my throat stopped feeling sore.

I had only been home about half an hour when Mrs Jackson, the elderly lady from next door, came across to see me. She asked to see my throat, being curious to see what had been done, and after a nod from Mum I dutifully opened my mouth for her to inspect it. Just before leaving she told us she had a bit of a cold and had the audacity to warn me about getting near to people with colds and coughs until I was better. Too late. The following day I started sniffing and by the end of the week I had a full blown cough and cold. The infection had caught me as quickly as that. When the doctor visited he was not at all pleased. He gave me a long lecture on healthcare and keeping my distance from cold carriers. Mum and I exchanged glances behind his back. We were both to blame for my condition. He prescribed the usual antibiotic tablets and another week from school. In all I had a total of three weeks off instead of the original one. I had not missed much schooling by the time I returned and a few evenings of extra homework soon allowed me to catch up.

Did the operation do the trick? No of course it didn't. I still managed to catch the various viruses that circulated the school. When I recovered from the operation and the convalescing period I returned to my normal routine and the visits to the church and youth club. While I had been absent the youth club leaders had organised weekly bicycle rides into the country. They met once a week during the summer months, rode out to a specific village or beauty spot and, if there was somewhere to take refreshment, had a short break and returned to the church to disperse. I thought it a great idea and longed to join them but unfortunately I did not possess a bicycle. As things stood at the time I was unable to buy one and my parents were not in a position to help me out financially. I was offered the loan of a cycle one evening but, not wanting the members of the youth club to be aware of my financial situation, said that I was saving for one of my own and declined the offer. I knew it would not be that year anyway.

Towards the end of that particular summer Dad surprised me by saying that one of the factory workers had a lady's cycle for sale, second-hand of course. Five pounds was the asking price and Dad said he could afford that if I was interested. Interested? I was full of enthusiasm. The day it was delivered I could not get home from school fast enough. When I saw it propped up against the wall in the gateway I could not believe my eyes. I nearly died. It was not at all as I imagined. It was a lady's cycle all right but one of the old-fashioned 'sit up and beg' type, very Victorian with large wheels. When I sat on the saddle and held the handlebars, I was sitting very straight backed, hence the name. I could not help but show my disappointment but eventually, when it subsided, I told Dad it was fine. It was a bike and much better than missing out on the trips with my friends. I knew they would probably have a good laugh at my expense because most of them had the sporty or normal upright cycles.

Dad checked the bicycle, the tyres and brakes. He painted it black where there were scratches and signs of wear. He fitted a bell to the handlebars. When he declared it fit to ride on the roads, I waited eagerly for the next evening cycle trip with my friends. To my amazement when I arrived on it they passed no comment or laughed. Perhaps they were being kind as I was beginning to see the funny side myself. Despite sitting high and upright in the saddle, I was able to pedal as fast as the next person and managed to keep up with the group, losing myself among the central circle of cyclists. Now able to join in wholeheartedly with the group, I spent many happy evenings on treasure hunts and obstacle rides, covering quite a distance in a couple of hours. I recall the longest ride was about 25 miles when our leader for the evening took a wrong turning, and we cycled on oblivious to the fact for several miles before we halted and found a new way back to the original route. I arrived home exhausted and very late. It was dark and having no lights I knew my parents would be anxious. I remember cycling fast, standing up on the pedals as I whizzed down the hill on East Park Road from the Evington Cinema to Gwendolen Road, avoiding the old tram lines that were still along the main road. Mother nearly lost her temper because she thought something had gone amiss and I had had an accident. Little did she know how near to one I had been during that hell for leather ride home. She banned me from any further cycling trips as a punishment for being late. Dad gave me a lecture about riding a cycle in the dark without lights. I said nothing and realised it was best to accept the chastisement and to make sure it did not happen again. Mother argued that I should have been more observant and not rely on others. Well, by the end of the week she had relented. Dad fixed a lamp on the front and a small red lamp to the rear. Both were battery driven and I had to make sure they were working before leaving home, and lit as soon as daylight began to fade.

I kept the cycle clean and in good condition. Dad serviced it for me periodically and inspected the chain. It was always well oiled and I had to be careful not to get the thick black oil on my skirts. There were numerous occasions when I caught my calf on the chain and had a long smudged black oil mark that only came off after being rubbed with butter or lard. It took some removing.

One day Dad gave me a puncture repair kit to put in the small leather pouch that hung from beneath the saddle at the rear. Only once was I unfortunate to have a puncture while out in the country lanes and one of the lads was good enough to repair it for me so that I could get home on time.

The cycle gave me great freedom of movement. Not only did I have the company of the youth club on the evening trips, but I was able to go solo on numerous occasions. This enabled me to explore the surrounding area of my home. I recall one such ride when I dared to cycle alone along Broad Avenue for the first time. This road and Coleman Road were very rural at the time and, with only the City General Hospital standing in the middle of fields, it was a very lonely area to explore alone. I had been told that the local name for Coleman Road was Cut Throat Lane because a young woman had been found murdered with her throat cut many years previously and the murderer never traced. Passing all the trees, hedges and bushes, I cycled at great speed to get past the thickly wooded area and around the country lanes to Evington village.

On another occasion I cycled out on the country roads to Scraptoft Village, Keyham Lane and Thurnby. In the fields were still many Italian prisoners of war wearing their dark brown battledress uniforms. They worked on the hedgerows and on the farms. Some waved as I passed but I dare not stop. I never told Mum about these expeditions for fear of being banned from taking cycle rides alone.

The cycle turned out to be my best friend over the years. I was always sorry I had ridiculed it when it first arrived. It was sturdy, kept in good condition and always reliable. I rode it until it began to drop to pieces with age. Dad eventually broke it up and disposed of the pieces at the council tip. I promised myself I would save up for another more modern version, but I never seemed to get around to it. My 'sit up and beg' cycle was my one and only.

Dad was very good at giving surprises and after the cycle he followed it up by presenting me with something I had always yearned to possess. The previous winter, 1947, had been extremely severe with snow that had fallen fast and thickly. In a short time it had covered the countryside, caused many places in Britain to be snowbound, and was hazardous for weeks. Roads were blocked and villages were cut off until the snowploughs cleared and forced their way through to bring relief.

We children thought it was marvellous and took every opportunity to have fun and games in the snow. Of course we all had to do our part by sweeping the pavement outside our front doors, piling the snow into the road but leaving a gap along the gutter for when the thaw set in and the roads became awash with water. Periodically there was a break in the snow piles to allow pedestrians to cross the road. When our chores were completed we were able to take advantage of the nice clean snow on the park. Living very near to Spinney Hill Park, I spent a long time watching the sledges racing down the icy slope from Mere Road to East Park Road. There were two slopes. The first ran the full length of the park and was used by the teenagers and adults experienced in the use of the dangerous icy run. It was about thirty feet wide and in the severe cold conditions soon became a complete sheet of ice. Sledges travelled at dangerous speeds and were steered at the last moment into soft snow, halting within a few feet of the unfenced frozen brook.

The second slope, the nursery slope, ran from the bandstand down to the cricket pitch and was half the length of the other. It was mainly used by children and learners. A far safer slope. I was fascinated and dearly loved the idea of travelling smoothly down the slopes on a sledge. Several times I had asked Dad to make me one but because Mum had seen the state of the major run and the speed that the sledges reached she objected, reasoning that the slopes were unsafe for youngsters of my age and she feared for my safety. However, I worked on Dad and the following winter after a very heavy fall of snow I was suddenly presented with a beautiful home-made sledge. Dad had excelled himself in woodwork. It was well made with sturdy wood, the runners were well greased, and a strong cord had been threaded through holes near to the footrests. I was ecstatic and could not wait to try it out. I had to listen to a lecture from Mum about safety and was made to promise never to use the main slope. So keen was I to take part in this wonderful sport that I would have promised anything. So while there was some snow about I ran to the park and rode the small slope at every opportunity. It was great fun. One day I decided that the main slope did not look too dangerous and plucked up courage to have a go. I forgot all about my promise in my enthusiasm.

I queued up at the top of the hill to take my turn. Then, making sure I had a good grip on the cord, pushed myself forward and rode down the slope at the side of the icy run. I gathered speed until I held my breath with fright. There was nothing I could do but hold on and steer straight. Other toboggans whizzed by with their crazy riders shouting and waving to their friends as they seemed to fly across the thin ice.

I held on tightly and felt the wind whistling through my woolly hat, biting into my cheeks and ears. Pulling tightly on the cord, I leaned back pressing my wellington boots hard onto the footrests and stared through squinting eyes as I literally flew down the slope. I had no control over the sledge. Stopping was going to be a problem and I had not anticipated my speed. The sledge had fixed steering so to veer to one side to avoid the brook was nigh impossible. Suddenly, the error of my action struck me and I saw only one way out. As the trees in front of the brook loomed

before me and my speed did not decrease, I let go of the cord, leaned back and rolled off the sledge into soft snow. It was a jolt and I rolled over several times before stopping. I was unhurt. The sledge, having lost its weight and being tipped to one side, veered to the right and hit one of the large trees. There was such a smack. The sledge did a couple of somersaults before landing upside down inches from the edge of the brook. My heart pounded. It had been a near miss. But what a ride! The exhilaration and thrill left me gasping. It also frightened me out of my wits. I dare not chance a second ride. Fortunately, the sledge was none the worse for striking the tree and only showed the usual wear and tear marks. I was glad I had made the run but it was a secret I kept to myself. I could not boast about it for fear of my parents getting to hear of it. I knew they would ban me for life.

That same evening, on the front page of the *Leicester Mercury* was the story of a young man, aged twenty one and the son of a policeman, who had been killed the previous day on Spinney Hill Park. He had ridden his toboggan down the main slope at speed and crashed into one of the large trees at the bottom. He was killed instantly. That did it. No more sledging for me. The weather changed shortly afterwards and the sledge was put away for another year. It was only used in the snow to haul Julie along the pavement or on the park in snowy weather. I never rode the slopes again.

Moving images

1949 was to be the year I left school and it would pass quickly enough. However before that great day arrived in July, I was to remember the year for several reasons. Firstly, it was the year that Dad and I became more interested in football and supported the local team. Most Saturday afternoons found us down at the Filbert Street ground cheering on the Leicester City team with thousands of other supporters. We would queue up for the terrace, and in all weathers stand among ardent supporters shoulder to shoulder. Blue and White, the City colours were everywhere we looked. A great cheer would sound when the team ran onto the field to the strains of *The Post Horn Gallop* played on a horn by a man dressed in hunting pink.

On the days City played badly the crowd would jeer, curse and swear. Dad often steered me through the crowds to a better position, away from the obscene language that was let out after some misdemeanour by a player or in respect of the referee who it seemed, was always in need of spectacles. Eventually I learned to ignore the remarks and the language. After all, I pointed out to Dad, it was a man's game and if we women were present then we had to put up with it.

1949 was a good year for the City. They fought well in the rounds of the F.A. Cup and managed to win their way to the final at Wembley. The match was in April and they were to play Wolves. We knew we would not be going but, to rally support, I made several large blue and white rosettes to wear on our coat lapels on the day of the match. We planned to listen to every move the teams made over the radio. However, this was the year that a great many homes in the south of England could watch the match on television for the first time. Dad had an ex-naval friend, Ernie Doyle, who lived with his wife Edie and their small daughter Barbara in North Street, Isleworth, just outside London. He received an invitation by letter to visit and stay overnight, specifically to watch the match on their television. Dad was thrilled and, when the day came, pinned his rosette on his coat and travelled down to London on the train with all the other supporters. Mum and I were to listen to the match on the radio. City lost. We looked forward to Dad's report of his trip. He was so thrilled he could hardly wait to get indoors to tell us about it. What a weird and wonderful thing it was. He kept us in suspense as he related every step from arriving at their home to leaving. He told us that the house was full of men who had been invited to watch the match on the small television in the lounge. Dad described how the set was held in a large, dark brown cabinet with the television set into the top half. The screen measured nine inches square and the picture was black and white. Constantly there were white flashes and a muzzy picture but the cameras followed every move the players made. He reckoned it was better than actually being at Wembley. He said that they sat in the darkened room hardly speaking, then cheering a good pass or a goal. During the match Edie served sandwiches and drinks. It really was a very special occasion. Dad reckoned it would not be long before every home had a set and when it came to Leicester he would consider having one.

My sister was about ten years old when we indulged ourselves and rented a television from the Radio Rentals

Captains Billy Wright (Wolverhampton Wanderers) and Norman Plummer (Leicester City) lead their teams out onto the pitch at Wembley for the 1949 FA Cup Final (Neville Chadwick Photography)

Shop in High Street, Leicester. At that time, many people bought sets then found to their dismay that the tubes blew and cost a lot of money to be replaced. Dad considered the renting of a set more economical until the sets were improved sufficiently to last without any attention.

When the television set was installed in our living room we were just as amazed as Dad had been. We could not believe that the pictures were coming through the air. From then on the radio took a back step. No longer was I ironing on a Monday evening listening to *Dick Barton Special Agent* or *Journey into Space*. There were no more frights from Valentine Dyall, the *Man in Black*, with gruesome tales of murder and intrigue. Now it was television plays and variety, with intervals long enough to make a cup of tea. Intermissions between programmes showed the Potter's Wheel and *From London to Brighton in Three Minutes*, a fantastic train ride. All were interesting and fascinating, despite the white lines that flashed and the frequent losses of picture. The weather appeared to interfere with the picture many a time, causing tiny flashing white spots or lines that ran from top to bottom. It was not necessary to use our imagination as we did listening to the radio. Now it was pictures showing everything, just like a film at the cinema. The news and weather programmes were a must each evening and we stopped what we were doing to watch. We had our favourite programmes such as *What's My Line*, *Juke Box Jury* and *Sunday Night at the London Palladium*. My sister, growing up with television, accepted it as normal and watched programmes more suitable for her age. I think her favourites were the serials like *The Railway Children*, *Kidnapped* and *The Prince and the Pauper*.

Eventually Mother put her foot down. We were watching too much and it seemed to be taking over all our leisure periods. She would only let us watch certain programmes or have a family conference as to what we would watch together, then it was switched off until the next choice. How the television has changed since then.

The second memory of 1949 was more serious. The cinema had released documentary films about the Jewish death camps and the atom bombing of Japan. Although they were part of a cinema programme and months apart, I forget the feature films we saw but recall these documentaries quite clearly. These films made me sit in stunned silence with everybody else in the cinema and, afterwards, all the people left the cinema quietly, some weeping.

The first film was of the concentration camps at Belsen and Auschwitz. I recall seeing the death camps with the pits of dead and mutilated bodies. Then there were the walking dead in their grey and black striped, ragged uniforms. Skeletons covered with filthy rags. I saw the German guards, men and women in their uniforms, their mouths and noses covered with cloth masks to keep out the smell from the decomposing bodies as they threw skeleton-like corpses, all naked, into great lime pits. I remember the faces of those men, women and children who were fortunate enough to have survived the horrors, who were standing or squatting on the ground, unable to believe that the allies had arrived to rescue them. Their eyes showed much suffering and were empty of any emotion. They were unable to move or accept they were free from the terrible regime of the camp.

As the years went on, the truth about the concentration camps came out to the public. The barbaric and horrific cruelty, the experiments, and the way the Jews were gassed and disposed of in their millions while in the hands of the Germans, was hard to believe. Mother said that it showed the worst examples of how humans could inflict such terror on another race of people, and that we should never forget the atrocities that had taken place during the war.

The next film I saw caused me even more distress and I was very frightened. It concerned the dropping of the atomic bombs on Hiroshima and Nagasaki. Both caused great devastation and death to thousands, but brought the war with Japan to an end very quickly. The documentary started by showing how the monster bomb was created and the history of the making of the weapon. Then came the politics and the decision to use it. I felt little emotion as this part of the film unfolded, then the loading of the bombs onto the American planes. I watched quietly and unmoved as the plane flew over Japan and located its target. The bomb door slowly opened and away went the bomb in complete silence. Then I saw the mighty explosion and heard some of the noise. A great fireball followed and an enormous mushroom shaped cloud of smoke and debris rose into the air. Next came the pictures of what remained of Hiroshima. There was nothing there! It was completely devastated. Flattened rubble, burnt black in seconds. I gasped when I saw that nothing remained. Then came the terrible photographs of the injured and dying. The dead it seemed were the lucky ones. I remember the pictures of a small Japanese man standing facing us. His front looked quite normal but when he turned around, he was burnt black right to the bone from head to feet. How he remained standing was a miracle. I recall staring in horror. A child was shown who had held its arms across the chest at the time and it was burnt all the way down the front except for the cross made on the body where the arms had protected it. The sights of people walking about with their skin dropping off, and others with the pattern of their wearing apparel tattooed on their skins and bodies, was sickening. The pictures shocked me. This film was one I was never to forget.

It did not seem possible that we, the supposed civilised portion of the world, who classed ourselves above those atrocities caused by the Germans could have caused such horror on Japan. As time passed, we were to learn of the long term effect that the bombs had on the human life, as people in their thousands died agonising deaths caused by the fallout.

My mother was right to take me to see these films and I have never forgotten them. It would have been easy to walk out of the cinema and accept it as political propaganda, not knowing just to what lengths a certain race would stoop in the name of ethnic cleansing and keeping the peace. Many people objected to the films being on general release, and although I have seen many films on the subject since, there appears to have been little restriction or censorship, as only a small portion of what I remember seeing at the time is seen on the television today.

As a young impressionable teenager, I was shocked and understood only too well the wholesale destruction that could be caused by one atom bomb, and realised it must have been a warning to mankind. Even used in defence against another warring nation, it could easily wipe out the human race in a few minutes. I also knew that the threat of a nuclear bomb would be held over our heads for the rest of our lives, as other countries began to produce nuclear weapons, all in the name of keeping the peace.

In addition to the films, in April 1949 the last of the Nuremberg Trials, after three and a half years of courtroom drama, came to an end. The Nazi leaders, still alive but responsible for war crimes, the deaths of millions of Jews, the torture and concentration camps, were eventually found guilty of their crimes against humanity and were sentenced to death, life imprisonment or varying lesser sentences. The whole issue, with photographs and films, had been front page news and had brought back to me all the sickening facts again. I became fearful for the future and wondered what steps would be taken to make certain nothing like it ever happened again.

1949 was also a memorable year for Dad. He worked with a friend at the Standard Engineering factory who secured a job working for the East Midlands Electricity Board at the power station on Raw Dykes Road. He spoke of the increase in wages, the opportunities open to ex-naval engineers and of the vacancies available. Dad was interested. He set about making enquiries which led to an interview. It meant a return to shift work but the pay was good and he accepted a post as a turbine driver, a very experienced and responsible job. He was employed at the power station for 21 years before being given compulsory retirement at the age of 64. He received a small sum of redundancy and an even smaller weekly pension. However, he had been satisfied with his work despite all the drawbacks living in Nottingham Road.

School's out

Two years at the Junior Art and Craft School flew by, and although putting off the decision of a future career or occupation until a later date, it suddenly loomed up in front of me before I knew where I was. I had enjoyed all the subjects and found drawing and craft enthralling. We were encouraged to illustrate our basic subjects with diagrams and drawings, and I remember submitting two papers that received excellent marks.

The first paper was on the muscles of the body and was to be accompanied by a full-length pencil drawing of the body's muscle arrangement. Copied from a book on the subject, I received great praise and a written compliment from the teacher. The second project consisted of several pencil and pastel drawings of Tudor costumes to illustrate and accompany the essay on the six wives of Henry the Eighth.

The art teacher was rather eccentric when it came to drawing from still life. She organised several trips into the county and city, to stand leaning on walls in small groups drawing a set piece that she thought interesting and within our capabilities. However, there were two occasions when she left us dumbstruck as to what she intended us to draw.

The first was a visit to the cattle market on Aylestone Road. We were conveyed to the establishment in a hired Corporation bus and then we disembarked at a point not far from the main entrance, among lorry loads of cattle, mooing quite loudly, obviously knowing of their impending doom. But we were not there to draw live animals, it was a visit to the Abattoir. What she thought we would find to draw heaven knows, but when we discovered our ultimate destination we showed our disgust and refused to put pen to paper. Not to be outdone, she indicated the wonderful ornate black iron gates at the entrance on Aylestone Road and we stood in a line opposite them, drawing away quite

(V. Tedder)

59

happily until the bus arrived about an hour and a half later to take us back to school for lunch.

The second visit was on a murky damp day when we walked from the school to the army barracks on Saffron Lane, South Wigston. We were instructed to draw what we could see from the road. I think she contemplated guns and tanks, sandbags and army equipment on show around the barrack square, but when we arrived there were only the brick buildings and army married quarters in the background. Everything was behind the high wire security fencing and there was not a soldier in sight. We giggled and drew whatever took our interest but it was really a waste of time. She was an accomplished artist herself and very encouraging when it came to our individual style.

The mathematics teacher had us walk around the school in pairs measuring walls, doors and windows in order to illustrate how much wallpaper we would require for a room or the length of material needed for curtains. We were given individual projects. Mine was to make a scale model of the Ritz Cinema on Blaby Road, South Wigston, from thick white card. I enjoyed the exercise. It was very educational and entertaining.

The domestic science teacher, who encouraged us to design an outfit, make it and wear it for the end of term exhibition, was very strict. She was in charge of the cooking and housewifery. Over the two years we were taught the basics of housekeeping. We were instructed on household chores, washing, starching, ironing and cooking. We baked cakes and cooked three course meals. The kitchen was equipped with modern stoves and utensils, all spotlessly cleaned before we were allowed to go home. It was a pleasure to learn to cook.

The music teacher, a lovely elderly lady, was very keen for us to appreciate music. A good pianist, she spent many hours in the school hall seated at an upright piano playing her favourite pieces. The sound of rousing marches, polkas and waltzes filled the school at any time of the day, broken only by the young voices of girls practising for the Open Day at the end of term. I was one chosen for the choir. We were asked who were in church choirs before being selected. There was no volunteering or trying to back out. Once in the school choir, there you stayed until the end of school days. We spent many hours practising scales and holding the notes. As the Open Day drew near we participated in extra practices after school hours. We were coached through several songs until two were thought to be within our capability. None of us were good singers or had received any tuition or special training, but we were expected to perform all the scales and breathtaking long notes that made up the music to *Nymphs and Shepherds*. We held our breath until we exploded into giggles. She brought us back to order by playing a heavy cord on the piano. Sometimes she had to strike it more than once before we stopped.

The second song committed to memory was *The Trout*, not such a hard number to master. Eventually with much patience on the part of the teacher we performed these two pieces with credit. However, we were nothing in comparison to professional choirs.

I made good progress at school and ended up being top of the class and the runner up in the examinations. It was decided that I had been a late developer and intelligent enough to warrant further education. The Headmistress summoned me to her office and arranged a date for my parents to attend the school to discuss my future. She was of the opinion that my schooling should continue until the age of 18 years. It was a waste of time because I knew Mother was totally committed to me earning my living as soon as possible. When I gave the Headmistress's message to my parents they listened and, after a moment's thought, poured forth the excuses. It meant purchasing another uniform, more sports kit, educational needs, books and sundries. They felt that Dad's small wage could not take on the extra cost. I liked being at school but knew it had to end. In fact the thought of attending the chosen school rather frightened me when I discovered all the subjects to be learned to obtain the Certificate of Education. For a time it was just a dream, especially as I did not know what sort of career to follow.

To soften the blow my parents indicated that they were pleased with the way I had progressed from my poor educational beginning, but after great deliberation decided it was too much of an expense. They told me that the time had come for me to go to work and start contributing towards the family budget.

The good part of my life came to an end when school finished for the summer in July 1949. On the last day I took part in the fashion show wearing my new dress for the first time. I had styled the dress with short sleeves, a round neckline and a gathered skirt onto a basque at the waist. The material was thin rust coloured wool that unfortunately stretched easily and was difficult to sew. The neckline was cut rather low at the front and in desperation I sought help from Mum. She suggested the neckline would appear higher and smaller by inserting some cream lace along the edge. I did just that, and when it was finished it was well disguised. I paraded along the catwalk, fully conscious of my mistake and sure it was noticeable to everyone. Hurrying from the catwalk and anxious to remove the offending dress, the sewing mistress gave me a smile of appreciation and bade me return to take a bow to loud applause. At the end of the afternoon was the prize giving. My form teacher, a tall thin woman with straight hair who talked a little aside like a Shakespearean actor, handed me a prize. In front of the whole school she praised me on my achievement and handed me a book. It was my one and only school prize. I had received many from Sunday school for good attendance, but a prize from school was really something to be proud of. The book, *Birds, Trees and Flowers*, produced by Odhams Press Limited, contained wonderful illustrations, drawings and charts contributed by famous authors. Inside the front cover was a special certificate issued by the City of Leicester Education Committee. Beautifully written in bold black ink was my name and the reason for the prize - Good Work, 1949. I was so excited and thrilled I ran from the hall to take refuge in the cloakroom and have a quiet weep. It had been so unexpected.

That was the end of my school days. At the age of 15 years I wondered what I was going to do for a living. The carefree days were over and there was no one to guide me. My decision to leave school was accepted without comment and further interest in me was gone. All I had to my credit was the fact that I was good at drawing, art, domestic science and sewing. There were no diplomas or certificates to prove my worth. The G.C.E. A levels system did not yet exist in my school era. It seemed therefore, that the only occupation left available for me was something in the sewing line. So with no qualifications I sought work as a dressmaker in a factory. At least, I thought, it was a start. I had ideas of specialising and eventually running my own business but until then I had to learn the trade and the routine of fashion productivity. Somehow I meant to better myself in the future. The long hours bent over a sewing machine did not appeal to me. In the meantime I elected to accept my lot and searched the local press for a suitable job. Mother forestalled me by telling me that she had heard of a job at Martha Hill's factory on St Barnabas Road, where a junior was required as a runabout with a view to learning the trade. It was not far from home and the firm had a good reputation. She suggested I went along to make enquiries.

Martha Hill's firm was well known for the manufacture of ladies woollen garments. It was a leading fashion house for *Ladies Pride* wear, which were made on the premises and sold all over the British Isles. It sounded a good place to start work and possibly progress to higher things.

I was rather taken aback at the interview when the forelady, a sergeant major type in a blue overall, stood towering above me and told me the conditions of work. The hours were long, 8am to 6pm five days a week with one hour for lunch. I would be a runabout for a few weeks until I learned the layout of the factory and some of the sewing machine skills. I was to be under strict supervision until she thought I was ready to work a machine. The weekly wage was the princely sum of one pound and five shillings. I dreaded starting work. The glamour had gone out of it. Full of despondency and unable to say no to the job, I agreed to start work at 8am on the second Monday in August. In the meantime I was to celebrate leaving school by taking a week's holiday. It was the August bank holiday week when every factory in Leicester closed.

I returned home and told my parents the news that I had accepted the job, the hours of work and the weekly wage. Mum arranged with me that in view of the poor starting rate she would take the one pound and give me the five shillings for pocket money. She would buy my clothes when they were needed. She was of the opinion that the prospects of advancement at the firm were good and that the small wage would only be for a short time. I accepted the arrangement she had made although I was not too happy about it. As it turned out, she looked after my needs well. Only time would tell whether the firm would come up to expectation.

Then, putting all thoughts of work out of my mind I prepared myself for a holiday with my godmother. I arranged to travel down to stay with my godparents at Rainham in Kent for the week. I liked my godparents and looked forward to their company.

My godmother, Ruby Gibson, her husband Ron and their two children, Joy aged 19 years and Roger about 13 years, lived in a detached house at the top of a hill. At the side of the house was a large playing field and school. I had often played in the field on short visits during the war when Mother and I made trips to see Dad after his ship docked at Chatham for repairs or to take on supplies. I thought the house was wonderful, with well tended gardens back and front and a large lawn at the rear on which to play. At the top of the staircase was a window and on a clear day the view was magnificent. Across the

fields and the valley of Rainham we could see the river and The Medway in the distance.

Auntie Ruby was a lovely person, always ready to help and explain things. She was a chatterer but had very interesting things to say. She was slim, extremely good looking with beautiful, light brown wavy hair. She was a chain smoker. Uncle Ron was the opposite in temperament. A quietly spoken man, tall and very thin. He never appeared to get upset with anything or anyone. He was employed at the dockyard and we saw very little of him while we were there. He adored his children and nothing seemed too much trouble to make them happy.

Joy was a redhead like her father and her hair was the envy of all. It shone with natural waves and there never seemed to be a hair out of place. She was very attractive and was chased by all the local lads. She worked at the oil refinery on the Isle of Grain, and over the years the fumes from the oil that saturated the air, gradually took the colour from her hair and it turned a dark reddish brown, losing some of its lustre. However, she was great fun and we had many hysterical escapades.

I slept in a double bed with her and we would lie awake for hours chatting and giggling about this and that. I recall on this particular visit that she was having some trouble with a boyfriend. He wanted to have a serious relationship leading to an engagement and marriage, but she couldn't decide whether this was what she wanted. She contemplated giving him up altogether but was unsure what steps to take. At 15 with no experience of men whatsoever I became her confidant and advisor. I listened, told her my point of view, gave what I thought I would do in the circumstances from my experience of men, and left her to make her own decision. It took her the whole of the week, much to my satisfaction, in which she decided to have a complete break from seeing him and devote her time to me.

We took country walks, went shopping in Chatham High Street, in Rainham and Gillingham and visited the beautiful local Downs. We walked the dogs, an Alsatian and a Pekinese, and had a couple of visits to the cinema. One cinema visit was an outing I have never forgotten. Joy, Roger and I set off one afternoon for the local cinema matinee. I cannot remember the main feature film but the accompanying B film was hilarious. It was *Things Happen at Night*, or a similar title, and I recall it starred Gordon Harker. It was an old black and white comedy with frequent, silly and amusing exploits by Harker and his band of friends. The funniest part was when he used a fly spray to ward off some unwanted guests. It was one of the old-fashioned cylinder shaped fly sprays which had a long handle. To squirt out the liquid he had to pump the handle up and down. During the film the fly spray was squirted at all and sundry and we went into hysterics. We laughed until we cried. Then we laughed all the way home, choked over our teas and at every opportunity burst out laughing. It was useless trying to suppress it. I gasped for breath several times and held my aching waist. Auntie Ruby ordered us to stop but she only made matters worse. At bedtime, thinking we had got over it, we started again. In the night we awoke to giggles from Roger in the next room and that started us all off again. We just could not get it out of our system and we continued to have bursts of hysterics for the rest of the week.

On the following Saturday my parents and Julie arrived to collect me. They were staying overnight and we were to travel back to Leicester on Sunday. On the Saturday afternoon, Mum and Dad left Julie with us while they went into Chatham to do some shopping. When they returned they presented me with a present - a wristwatch. I thought it was a wonderful gift. The watch face was pink and the hands and figures a blue-black colour. It had a narrow black leather strap. It was my very first watch and I treasured it for years. It was a Sunday best watch. I never dare wear it for work in case I scratched the face on the machinery or damaged it in any way. Receiving the watch was the climax to a wonderful holiday. What memories it gave me. The

following Monday morning I was to start work.

I recall not mentioning to my friends that I had taken a job in a factory. I seemed to feel it was rather unbecoming being a factory girl after all that had been said about me receiving further education and being top of the class.

I thought that starting work would put an end to the paper round days, but the small starting wage I was paid made me decide to keep it on for a few months to help out with the pocket money. The days would certainly be longer in these circumstances. Up at 6.45am, newsagents for 7am, deliveries between then and 7.45am and then straight to work for 8am until 6pm. Looking back, I really did earn my small weekly income.

I started work, when the time came, wearing my old school summer dresses and the faithful maroon cardigan. I was advised to make myself some large aprons to wear at the factory to keep the fluff and cottons off my clothes. Also, to treat myself to a pair of dressmaking scissors, which I was advised never to lend to anyone. To make sure they were always in my possession, I tied them to a long piece of tape attached to my apron and made a large pocket in which to place them when I had to leave the machine for any reason. Not that they would have been stolen, but a strange hand cutting with them could have spoilt the sharpness.

Starting work was to be a great adventure. What would the future hold for me?

Clocking in machine and cards
(Leicester City Museums)

CHAPTER FOUR
Clocking in

On my first working day, I arrived at 7.55am. The premises were alive with men and women arriving to start work at 8am. The factory occupied two floors above the large Provincial Garage and took floor space across the whole of the corner block between Kitchener Road, Uppingham Road and St Barnabas Road. The large panelled windows overlooked the streets and gave good views along the length of the road on each side.

I followed the women towards the factory, along a huge arched gateway access in St Barnabas Road. Through a narrow door on the left hand side, we climbed a steep wooden staircase to the first floor. Some men and women went through a door on the first floor, and others continued up the well-worn wooden stairs to the second floor.

Within minutes of arriving at the small office at the top of the stairs on the first floor, and exactly at 8am, the door opened and in strode the forelady. She was tall, extremely smart in her clean, well ironed, well laundered blue overall. It had long sleeves, buttoned at the wrist and pulled slightly at the buttons across her chest. She looked me up and down and, without stepping into the office, still holding the door open with her hand, she instructed me to follow her. The door was nearly closed by the time I had collected my thoughts and crossed the room. She was almost through the second door opposite by the time I caught up with her. She was a bustling sort of woman and instantly generated a no messing about atmosphere. I followed her across the small landing to a second door and, when she opened it, the noise was terrific. It took a few seconds to take in the sight before me. The room was full of long work benches. Women sat on either side of the benches in rows of five with their heads bent over sewing machines.

A typical local factory scene in the 1940s (Leicester City Council)

The belts that ran the machines passed over wheels underneath the wooden benches that seemed to be right on top of their legs as they worked the treadle below. Other benches, only a short distance apart, housed the overlocking, hemming, button and buttonholing machines. At the far end of the room were the large industrial presses and finishing tables. Clouds of steam rose into the air as the women, with open necked blouses and their sleeves rolled up, brought the long pressers down on top of the garments and pressed a button on the handle to let out the steam. It was an amazing sight.

Within twenty minutes of arriving I had been shown where to hang my coat and had a conducted tour of the workrooms, upstairs and down. I was informed that I was the runabout for the workers, the forelady and the packers. I was to locate where everything was stored or stacked in order to fetch, carry and deliver within the factory without wasting time. In three weeks' time, when I had learned where everything was located and understood the system of the orders, I would be allocated a sewing machine to learn the trade.

It did not take long to learn where cottons, petersham, zips, buttons, tags and labels were stored. I assisted in the packing room and kept the women workers supplied with garments and sundries. I pushed and pulled full and empty skips and trolleys, and learned to escape the noise for a time by disappearing to the second floor on some pretext or other. In this large airy room I would watch the cutters at work. They laid the patterns on top of material, a dozen layers thick, then drew around them with blue dressmaking chalk. When they were satisfied that the patterns had been laid well, so that no material was wasted, they took hold of large black electric cutters with a cable connected to the circuit in the ceiling and cut around the chalk marks most expertly.

It was always hot in the workrooms and in the summer every window in the place was thrown open to let the air through. The electric lights were lit all the time and every machine had a spotlight. The lights, as big as upturned dinner plates, green on the outside and white on the inside, hung on long chains from the ceiling. There were numerous cobwebs along the walls and ceiling and it was great fun turning the lights upside down to see the spiders scurrying away to a darker corner. Everywhere there was coloured fluff and dust. The floors were swept daily but there were always cottons, pins and empty bobbins lying about.

One day when I was helping in the packing department I came across a nest of baby mice. They were pink in colour with bluish, skin covered eyes. There were about a dozen, all snug in between sheets of new brown paper. One of the men scooped up the whole sheet of paper and took it away to the boiler room. I felt rather sad at their fate but later, when many more such nests were discovered, I realised the necessity to dispose of them.

The firm had a clocking in machine situated near to the door as we entered the factory. Three minutes past the hour was all that was allowed. Anything over that and the worker was stopped a full quarter of an hour out of his or her wages. The clock, with a white face and black figures and hands, was fitted inside an oblong wooden box. In front of the clock was another wooden box with a brass-edged slit in the top. To record our clocking in and out times, we removed a buff coloured card with our names and works number typed on the top and placed it in the slit. When pressure was applied to the card it activated the machinery inside the box which printed out the time. Often women who were running late would shout and run from the rear of the queue to the front, knowing that time lost was money lost. At the end of the day we repeated the process before leaving the premises. This time if we were before 6pm we lost a quarter of an hour out of our wages for leaving early. On Friday evenings the cards were collected by the office staff and the hours calculated for the week's pay.

Six weeks had passed when I noticed a mechanic working on a sewing machine at the end of one of the benches. It took him several days to strip it down, clean and oil it, replace parts and adjust the stitch. He made sure that the thin leather belt which ran around the wheel, giving rotation to the treadle, was tight enough to give speed when treadling. When he had finished he covered the machine with a black material hood. It was my machine and was ready for use but I had to wait for the forelady to do the honours of showing me how to use it.

Three days later, under the supervision of an elderly lady named Rose, who was to work next to me, I was shown how to make up the garments. I learned how to put zips in dresses and skirts without having to change to a special foot each time, and to do the intricate stitching required round the collars and cuffs.

I enjoyed the work and learned my trade quickly. I was given garments in lots of a dozen at a time tied up in bundles direct from the cutters. I machined up the garments as quickly as I could. After a few months the forelady, who was not as bad as she appeared, sent for me and suggested that as I was well able to earn two pounds ten shillings a week on a regular basis I would be better off starting to work on my own time, or piece work as it was known. I was earning double my previous wages and even with payment of one shilling a week income tax I would be better off. As my speed and experience increased so my wages improved. From then on there was no messing about or disappearing to the second floor for a breather. Time was money.

I became quite an experienced lockstitch machinist but there was no training to further my career towards being a sample hand and working with the designers, and my ambition to improve my status was somewhat thwarted. In February the factory workers were put on short time. It was a bad month in the trade, I was told, being the end of the winter ranges and the lull before the new autumn designs appeared.

My week was suddenly cut from five days to three. I worked full pelt on these three days, Monday, Wednesday and Friday, from 9am to 4pm. It greatly reduced my wages and I was advised, as we all were, to sign on the dole for the odd two days. At least I would receive something to make up for my loss of earnings. I discovered the two days would bring me the princely sum of seven shillings and sixpence and my National Insurance Stamp. I had to attend the Youth Employment Bureau in Pocklington's Walk on both days to sign the appropriate form. This meant travelling into town on the bus as I had no other means of transport. I walked it a couple of times but it took most of the morning to get there and back.

My seven shillings and sixpence was paid out at 10am on the Friday morning, so I had to lose two hours of precious working time to go and collect it. It was a ridiculous situation and a system only youngsters under 18 years of age had to endure. Women over that age went once a week to sign on the dole, then received their payment by post office order through the post. They lost no working time at all. I put up with the inconvenience for three weeks, then decided to look for another job. I had heard that several similar factories were in full employment and it was stupid to continue on half wages when I could do better.

The forelady was none too pleased when I gave notice. I received a lecture on working for a living and how I had been taught the trade. She did not think I should leave and should have stuck it out for a few more weeks. I had to leave, there was no option. She did not have to survive on my small wages.

Without losing any time I secured a job at the Trafford factory in Lancaster Street, just round the corner from my home. The hours were the same and I was to start immediately on my own time. It was a good move, and when I told the new forelady of my ambition to work as a sample hand and with the designers, she said there was no reason why I should not do so. They were always on the look out for good sewers with good design ideas. I thought my chances of improving my status and being somebody would possibly come true at the Trafford. Only time was to tell.

The Trafford had a much better environment. It was larger, cleaner and lighter. They played music while we worked in the morning and afternoon, and had a very considerate manager, Mr Pell, who supervised everybody. He was a good worker and extremely helpful to the employees.

The factory, all on the ground floor, had offices, design rooms, sales rooms and a modern canteen overlooking

Lancaster Street. In the factory area were the large cutting out tables, the making up machinery, the finishing department, and the pressing and folding area. Beyond that was another large room which consisted of the stores, materials and packing department. Men worked in this area, tugging and lugging the huge rolls of fabric, large bales of paper and packaging materials, and the boxes and parcels of finished garments stacked ready to be loaded into the vans for delivery to the shops and fashion houses. The vans and lorries had access to the factory at the rear in Jellicoe Road.

Down one side of the factory was a slanted roof, with long glass panels. These were periodically whitewashed during the year to give shelter from the heat of the sun. The whole place was light and airy with room to move between the benches. Inside, along the length of the machine room were situated the ladies' and men's cloakrooms. In addition, placed flat against the wall were dozens of small lockers, and each employee was allocated one against a number and key.

The moment I walked into the place I knew things would go right for me. I was made most welcome. My sewing machine was immaculate and ready for use. My position was in the centre of a row of ten machines, with five on each side. I had a machine which gave me plenty of room. Each machine was fitted with a small light but it was so light in the factory in the summer that I rarely used it. When it was raining or a rather dark day, the little lights would be switched on and heads would bend lower over the machines. The women on my bench were all married and very experienced. They taught me some quicker methods and how to cut corners to save time, always with piecework earning in mind. I was shown how to complete a dozen garments, making up twelve collars or cuffs at a time, all in an effort to increase speed. After a few months I was well on my way to earning four to five pounds a week but I had to keep up a good speed all day. I welcomed overtime on a Saturday morning from 8am to 12 midday when we were busy. It all helped to save for the little luxuries such as new shoes, clothes and holidays.

The firm had a similar clocking in and out system as my previous employers so I was used to it. I could not afford to have my hard earned pay deducted through bad timekeeping so I was never late.

During the first weeks I was taught overlocking, hemming and pin tucking. When work was short I was to put these extra trades to advantage and keep up my weekly earnings. Occasionally I was chosen to assist in the making up of a one-off garment, and under the instructions of the designers felt I was at last on the first rung of the ladder to being a sample hand. The few days it took getting the garment correct, by changing the style a little or altering a part slightly, and finishing the garment completely were on the firm's time. This meant there was no hurry and it did not matter how many times the garment was changed until it was perfect. If the new design caught the eye of a buyer there was work for everyone. I looked forward to the day of becoming a sample hand because it would be very interesting work and the experience would be invaluable. I was aware that the two sample hands already used by the firm received excellent wages and I was full of enthusiasm to follow in their footsteps. I did not take into account that it would probably take years. One woman, in her early forties, was a spinster and prepared to work until retirement and the other one, aged about 70 with no intention of retiring, were not much encouragement for me. The elder of the two indicated several times that she was not going to give up work while she could still carry on and the only way of getting rid of her was when she was carried out in a wooden box. Ah well!

My workmates around the bench were a mixed bunch. Mostly married women, they were pleasant and eager to assist a newcomer in the trade. Dorothy, a chain smoker, taught me a number of short cuts when machining garments. Smoking was not allowed on the factory premises and it was fascinating to see Dorothy taking her last deep draw of a cigarette before stubbing it out at the door just before she clocked in. At breaktime in the canteen, she smoked at least three cigarettes with her tea. When leaving off she had an unlit cigarette between her lips as she clocked out, stopping as soon as she reached the bottom step outside to light it. She did not smoke at all between these times, not even on a quick visit to the toilet. The forelady checked the toilets regularly and let it be known that anyone found smoking or having smoked in what was part of the factory premises, would be instantly sacked. It was a rule all smokers adhered to without complaint.

There were many changes of employees while I was there and the machine next to mine appeared the most frequently unoccupied. I did not mind as for a time I had extra space in which to work, and then a new face appeared which led to different conversations and a chance to learn other tricks of the trade.

One woman named Annie, who I shall never forget, started work as a part timer. She had children at school and worked from 9am until 4pm. Her appearance led one to think she was an elderly lady. Her hair was grey and parted in the centre right over the head. The hair was plaited each side and wound into a bun over each ear. The style was known as 'earphones' and extremely old-fashioned. She admitted she had worn her hair in this style for twenty odd years and that her family liked it. I found it hard to believe. She caused us quite a titter when she first arrived. Annie was a cuddly sort of person and quietly spoken. One day she amused and shocked us by saying that in her younger days she played piano at a local cinema. She was an accomplished pianist and played suitable music to accompany the silent films. We screamed with laughter one day when she gave us a demonstration by drumming her fingers along the edge of the workbench, swaying to accentuate the mood swings of the story. However, we were not to be deceived by her lively character. She was a scrat, working full-pelt all the time she was at work, always last into the canteen and first out after tea break. I envied her the speed by which she was able to plough through the bundles of garments until, one morning, the forelady summoned her over to her desk and chastised her for making up a number of garments wrongly. Not to be outdone, she took the garments home, unpicked them and on her own sewing machine put the garments right, returning them the next day completed properly. She lost no time at work or suffered loss of wages.

Among the garments to be made up were three inch square pieces of material used for the buttonholes. Also, strips of material about two inches wide by ten inches long which were machined onto the skirts as a backing for the zips. There were far too many pieces and the excess were discarded into a waste bag on completion of the garments. One day I mentioned these to Dad who thought it was an awful waste of material, especially as he could put them to good use. From then on I took home every piece that was not required and it was collected in a pillowcase. When Dad thought he had sufficient pieces, he pegged a small rug for the kitchen from the buttonhole pieces and a much larger rug for the living room from the pieces of leftover plackets. He used new hessian for the backing and pegged the pieces close together. These multicoloured rugs were heavy, serviceable, warm and lasted well. Over the years, while I was able to take home the surplus waste bits, Dad managed to peg several rugs for around the house.

Days out

Starting my day at 6.30am, completing my paper round and working all day until 6pm, did not leave me with a lot of energy in the evenings. Apart from a stroll to the allotment and perhaps the odd walk to Spinney Hill Park with my sister in the pram, my evenings were rather short. Occasionally there was an outing to the cinema or to the youth club, but early to bed limited the scope of social life. Weekends were looked forward to but even they were routine to a certain extent.

It soon became a habit to travel into Leicester to visit the retail market and purchase the week's greengrocery. After two hours checking the bargains and shopping sensibly I would stagger home under a very heavy load. One day I counted up the weight of my purchases and it was in the region of 20lbs. I must have been quite strong. There were occasions when I could afford a seat at the cinema in the city and went in the middle of a performance, carrying all the shopping. It spent most of the time at my feet once everybody was in and seated, but it was quite a commotion having to lift it onto my lap when anybody wanted to leave their seat for some reason. No one seemed to mind this inconvenience because the cinema was full of shoppers like myself. Sometimes, I took the shopping home, had a quick tea and ran to the Evington Cinema on East Park Road for the commencement of the performance at 7pm. It was a good, clean and cheap theatre. Best seats cost ninepence. Afterwards it was a run all the way home to be in for 10pm. Occasionally I stayed in to baby-sit while my parents treated themselves to a visit to the Evington Cinema, or I went with Mum while Dad did the honours.

Sunday also became routine in the summer months. I frequently helped prepare the Sunday lunch, often cooking it. I was quite a good cook because I had been preparing lunch and cooking it since the birth of my sister. In the afternoon, dressed in my Sunday best I walked to the Evington Road Church of Christ Sunday School for 2.30pm. I was in the bible class and our tuition took place apart from the others in the Vestry. It was a tiny room situated on a corner of the church, but very comfortable.

After tea, at about 5.30pm, Mum, Dad, Julie and myself would take a tram ride into Leicester to see and hear the Salvation Army Band. They met in the Market Place and held a short service before marching along Gallowtree Gate, around the Clock Tower and down Humberstone Gate to the citadel in Kildare Street. They were a smart group of people who played well and there was always plenty of people lining the route around the Clock Tower to see them pass by. If we arrived early enough, we took Julie into the Market Place and stood her on one of the stalls to see the band and there was always a few pennies for her to drop into the box. My father liked the Salvation Army, always having a good word to say about them. He had experienced their caring, helpful, down to earth attitude during the war and said that some of them had been very brave under severe war conditions. I agreed they were an excellent body of people, but I could not understand why they were so eager to go into public houses to make their collections when they were so ardently against drinking.

I recall that on one occasion when we went to the Market Place, Dad lifted my sister up onto a stall to get a better view when Mum noticed that her neck was swelling. We thought she had been stung or bitten because it came up so quickly, but she was not crying so it was not that. By the time we made a move to watch the band go by, her neck had swollen level with her ears and she had a temperature. We went straight home and summoned the doctor. When he arrived, he would not go anywhere near her, but sat in a chair on the opposite side of the room. He stated that there was no need for an examination, she was suffering from mumps. Poor Julie, she was poorly for a fortnight. Strange though, no one else caught it and we did

East Park Road and Chesterfield Road junction, late 1940s. (Leicester City Museums)

not know anyone who could have infected her. It is still a mystery where or from whom she caught it.

During the summer when the weather was good we often got up early, prepared sandwiches and a flask and caught the first tram into Leicester. We walked to St Margaret's Bus Station and queued up with hundreds more for the buses out into the country. There were long queues for Bradgate Park and extra buses were put on to allow for the increase in trade. I recall that everyone seemed orderly and were in a jovial mood. There was never any pushing or loutish behaviour. I also remember that the buses were not allowed to be full to capacity. There was always room to pick up extra passengers waiting at the stops along Sanvey Gate, Woodgate and Groby Road. We

usually arrived at the park around 12 noon, just in time for a drink in the garden of the Bradgate Arms at Newtown Linford before spending the rest of the day on the park. A marvellous day out and, if it was not too hot, we walked up to Old John for a magnificent view of Leicester and the surrounding countryside.

About 5pm we would join all the others making their way from the park to the bus stop outside the Bradgate Arms for the return journey. Sometimes there were so many people waiting for the buses that three or four others would be waiting further along the road. As each one filled up and pulled away so the next drew up at the stop. It was very orderly and we knew that we would get onto a bus at some stage. There were occasions when we

Julie watching Punch and Judy at De Montfort Hall gardens 1955 (V. Tedder)

behind high hedges lay the farm, a two story building with outbuildings and tall barns. There were sprawling gardens and flower patches at the rear of the house.

Aunt Ethel was pleased to see us anytime. We always arrived unexpectedly because they had no telephone and we usually made up our minds to visit on the spur of the moment after considering the weather.

We had great days and I would take my sister all over the farm showing her the chickens, letting her feed them and collect the eggs. We would stand in the cow shed and watch Uncle Fred, in his white overall and a white ex-navy cap cover over his head, milking the cows by hand while softly singing to them.

Before returning home, Aunt Ethel would prepare a grand tea in the farmhouse kitchen. It was a magnificent room, whitewashed from floor to ceiling and sparkling clean. There were great hooks in the ceiling which held hams, pieces of pork, chickens with their heads in white paper bags, and cheeses wrapped in muslin cloths.

She had home-made bread and cakes, preserves, pickles and wine stacked on the shelves in the cool adjacent larder. Our tea was very special. Before leaving, my parents were offered home-made parsnip wine which Mum said tasted more like whisky. Julie and I had fresh cold pasteurised milk in glasses, wonderfully cool and creamy. At last, the day over, we had to make our way back to Barwell to catch the Midland Red bus to Leicester. Before leaving, Aunt Ethel would give us a brown paper carrier bag containing eggs, cooked ham and something home-made from the larder. If we were a little late and Uncle Ted had the time, he would make room in the back of his van and drive us into Barwell. Often we waited while he brushed out the van and put down sacking covered with a blanket, so we could sit. Dad would ride in the passenger seat at the front. We would endure a rather uncomfortable bumpy ride along the country lanes for the short journey. After such a wonderful day Julie and I would arrive home in a tired state. Our shoes were filthy and our clothes

arrived for a bus at 5pm and did not arrive home until 7.30pm, or even after 8pm, but we did not mind. It had been a great day out.

There were visits to the family farm at Stapleton near Hinckley. It was owned by my great aunt Ethel and her husband Ted. It was an all day event when we visited on a Sunday. We prepared sandwiches and a flask and caught the first tram and later a Corporation bus into Leicester. After a short walk to the Southgate Street bus station we had a long ride through the villages to Barwell, usually arriving in time for a drink at the Blacksmith's Arms public house in the village square. Having suitably quenched our thirst we would start the two mile walk to Stapleton village. Aunt's farm was situated about three-quarters of a mile further on. There was no sign on the main road to indicate the farm. We walked along until we came to a great oak tree on the right hand side with a path through the field opposite. Across two fields, around a bend and

Humberstone Gate, Leicester (Leicester City Council)

covered in straw, mud and chicken feathers. We were never dressed properly for messing about on a farm. Dad would spend time washing and cleaning our shoes in a bucket of water in the yard. It was a grand experience and very exciting going to the farm, but unfortunately the visits were few and far between.

Bank holiday Mondays and Tuesdays were favourite days if the weather was fine. Armed with the picnic bag and flask of tea, we would take Julie in her pushchair and travel to the De Montfort Hall gardens. The Leicester Corporation arranged entertainment annually in the grounds, and if wet in the Hall. So it was an ideal place to be if the weather changed for the worse. There was always a large crowd in attendance. In between performances brass bands played lively music. I recall an Army band, the Kibworth Band and the Royal Argyle Pipe Band played there on several occasions.

Concerts were held outdoors in the auditorium sunk into the gardens at the side of the Hall. The stage looked quite small from the rear seats. These were dark green metal fold-up types and were set out in a semicircle facing the stage. They were raised on grass tiers. We could see the stage very well. The loudspeakers were excellent and we heard every word without it interfering with normal conversation.

Although there was a cafe inside the Hall, extra stalls were put in strategic places in the grounds to take the overflow of visitors. However, the majority of people took a picnic.

Variety shows were organised by a local man and he engaged many of the local talented artists to perform. Sometimes a well-known star was engaged to attract the crowds. There were young people from local dancing troupes, male and female singers, a musician, acrobats, jugglers, and a special comedian or clown to entertain the children. When he finished his act he invited the children onto the stage to perform tricks or to sing, and they would flock up the steps onto the stage. They were so keen to take part that the stewards stood guard and had to control the numbers.

In addition there was the Punch and Judy show which attracted a large circle of youngsters, who all joined in the heckling and shouting. Whatever was put on to entertain us, we had a very enjoyable day out.

For a change we sometimes went into town to see what was on offer in the way of day trips. Coaches would line up in Humberstone Gate near to the old weighbridge, with their destination written on a chalkboard resting against the front wheel. If the weather was favourable, we would take the usual picnic bag and be prepared to go anywhere that took our fancy, if there were seats available. We never booked in advance. These day trips were very popular. Usually, by the time we arrived at about 9.30am, the majority of coaches going on the long day trips to London or the seaside had left. We would stroll along the pavement outside the little newsagent's shop beneath the Secular Hall, reading the placards advertising the trips. There were crowds milling about making decisions and queuing for tickets. Most coaches left promptly at 10am. Much pushing took place among the late comers trying to secure their seats. Invariably the coaches left with a full load.

There were bus loads going to Wicksteed Park, Belvoir

Castle and many of the stately homes like Chatsworth House and Woburn Abbey. Then there were the coach trips to towns such as Stratford upon Avon, Oxford, Cambridge and Peterborough. Also there were the day or afternoon trips to Nottingham Castle and the evening mystery tours. We had plenty to choose from and we were never disappointed. Not having a car was not a disadvantage in those days, and the prices of the trips were very reasonable. We were able to go to most places by public transport, which was usually plentiful and frequent. The railway frequently ran special trains to the seaside for the day and we often took advantage of the cheap day returns.

Another show we attended each year was the City of Leicester Show held at Abbey Park. Armed for the day with plastic raincoats, umbrellas and the picnic bag, we would leave home early and head for Humberstone Gate

Julie and Mum looking into the pig pen at the Abbey Park Show (V. Tedder)

where a fleet of Corporation buses waited to convey the crowds down to the show. We chose to go on the second day as funds would not stretch to the opening day. Often it rained and sometimes it was cold and windy, but we went prepared. On wet days the mud around the tents had to be seen to be believed. So many people went in and out of the horticultural and flower marquees that bales of straw were stacked to one side of the entrances and were thrown down to mop up the water and mud. Wellington boots were a must on a doubtful day, especially if there had been a forecast of rain, because the trampling of feet soon turned these areas into a quagmire. The show was marvellous and every available space was occupied with something or other.

Julie and I were thrilled as we went from one tent to another, peering closely through the cage bars at the rabbits, pigeons, fowls, hamsters and the small farm breeds and pets. Apart from the occasional visit to Aunt Ethel's farm at Stapleton during the summer months, it was the only time we saw these animals and birds. The pigs, for obvious reasons, were housed in a pigsty outside, and were surrounded by children eager to pat the piglets or stroke the skin of the sow. Next to the pigs was a small area set aside for the display of rare breeds of cattle, sheep and goats. Tethered or led around the arena on a rope by men or women in white coats, the animals were stroked, examined and closely inspected by the judges before notes were made on a clipboard. We watched intently, choosing the animals we thought looked the best and finding that we knew nothing about the showing of these creatures as the coveted red, yellow, green or blue rosettes were awarded to another animal.

Julie was fascinated by the bees. We would spend quite a time at these displays. We watched the men in their specially designed protective gear enter the bee display tent, which was covered with a fine green net, and remove the honeycombs from the hives as the bees swarmed around them. However, we did not stay too long in this area just in case the bees descended upon us. I was a bit afraid they would find a hole in the net and escape.

On the entertainment side there were the thrilling events and acts performed in a special arena. Such daredevil skill, it was a wonder no one received serious injuries. The arena was oval shaped and set out on the grass beside the canal. It was roped off and had seats arranged at intervals around the perimeter. I recall one very spectacular performance that left us gasping with admiration. This was the show put on by the elite Cossack troupe. They wore dark trousers, shiny black knee high boots, and white silk shirts with full sleeves gathered tightly into a wristband. Gaily coloured cummerbunds were wrapped around their waists and brimless hats, made of fur or sheepskin and shaped like an upturned plant pot, were held tightly on their heads by black chin straps. The men would shout and call out as they rode across the arena at speed on their fine horses, and performed acrobatics from the saddle. Again at speed, they galloped across the arena collecting long handled spears driven into the ground at certain distances apart. With the spears gathered under one arm they would stop suddenly, rear the horses onto their hind legs and take a bow. Next came the picking up of coloured kerchiefs from the ground as they hung upside down in the saddle, or with one leg hooked through the stirrup and arms spread-eagled waving swords or ribbons. It was all very daring and exciting. They were extremely skillful and a talking point for weeks afterwards.

Another part of the entertainment I remember well was the large marquee erected for the purpose of dancing. It was a plain marquee with electric lights hung around the inside. The floor was covered with wooden panels slotted together and polished with white chalk. In one corner was the band, usually five or six musicians dressed in black trousers, white shirts, a coloured dicky bow and waistcoat. They wore straw boaters and played a mixture of instruments. There was a selection of music to dance to and Dad often took me around the floor in a waltz or quickstep. I would then sit out with Julie while he and Mum had a spin around the floor. There was always a crowd of people dancing, no matter what time of day. On wet days it was difficult to slide your feet across the floor because of the dampness and we laughed as we stumbled around.

The variety shows were held on a specially built stage near to the bowling green. Some of the performers we had seen previously at De Montfort Hall but we enjoyed them again. The show was watched from metal seats arranged in rows in front of the stage, or by sitting or standing on the grass. It was all good fun.

Often we made our way to the bandstand and ate our picnic sitting on the grass while listening to the regimental bands. The Royal Marines band was a favourite but other bands, the Army and Air Force, put on equally good programmes. Even at the bandstand the concrete area surrounding it was kept clear for those who wanted a dance or two.

Across the bridge on the Oval side of the park, usually set out for the cricket matches, was situated the dog show and the show jumping arena. There was plenty to see. A visit to the show was a success in another way for us because we met relatives and friends we had not seen for months. It was a great meeting place.

We never stayed for the fireworks display in the evening. After walking the park all day we were all very tired. At about 6pm, we would slowly make our way across the park towards the main entrance where Corporation buses would be waiting to take passengers back to the city centre.

Enroute to the bus, we would visit the food hall and the flower tents where preserves, food, wine, flowers and plants were offered for sale. Going to the show on the second day meant we were able to take advantage of the sale of produce at the end of the day. Everything was still fresh and sold quite cheaply. We filled our empty picnic bag with pots of home-made jam, small bottles of sample wines, cakes, cheeses and biscuits. In the flower marquee we purchased a bunch of prize winning but drooping flowers, and from the plant tent a small plant or cacti. Dad often sought the vegetable stalls and purchased a few prize kidney beans, carrots, cabbage or a cauliflower. Laden with this prize winning bounty and bundles of pamphlets and brochures we had collected throughout the day, we would board one of the buses, packed to capacity, back to the Clock Tower.

About 8pm we were home and could hear the fireworks display taking place on the park. We discovered that if we walked along Nottingham Road towards Jellicoe Road, we could see clearly the fireworks exploding in the sky. It was the climax of the day.

'Goodnight campers'

In the spring of 1950 Dad declared that we ought to have a proper holiday. We had to save and, with prudence and the pooling of our finances, we could afford one week in July. He had read about holiday camps and was eager to try that type of holiday. With my sister being three at the time he thought it ideal because of what they had to offer. Holiday camps were advertised as having comfortable family chalets, three meals a day, plenty of entertainment for all ages and a baby listening service.

At 15 I thought it a great idea. What an adventure. I

Dad (far left) in the line up for the 'knobbly knees' competition at Warners Holiday Camp, Hayling Island. (V. Tedder)

was eager to save. It would give me the opportunity to meet people of my own age.

Dad collected several brochures for Butlins, Maddisons, and Warners holiday camps. We spent hours pouring over the beautifully illustrated books, checking prices and dates. Eventually, after a family conference, we decided that Warners holiday camp at Hayling Island in Hampshire was the place for us. It was so exciting. Our first real family holiday together. Before booking, there was one most important job to be done. That was for me to get permission to take a week off work in July. The firm always closed down for the first week in August, Leicester bank holiday week, and everyone was expected to conform and take their holiday at that time.

I was kept waiting two days before the forelady sent for me. Permission was granted but I had to understand that I would lose my week's wages. Neither would I have a National Insurance Stamp for that week. I was advised to make arrangements for two weeks National Insurance to be stopped out of my wages the following week after I returned from holiday. I was only given permission because I was going away with my parents. If it had been with anyone else it would have been refused. I could not get home quickly enough that night to tell Dad the good news.

Within a couple of weeks the holiday was arranged and a deposit secured the booking. We were to travel by train and as I adored train journeys that alone would be a thrill for me.

For the next few months it was all we could talk about. I did as much overtime as possible to cover my loss of wages and to save for the holiday. Any extra money was handed straight to Mum, who was responsible for collecting and saving any extra cash.

When the great day arrived it was another adventure packing and getting ready. Mum packed Dad's ex-naval case, a green hard linen type with brown leather corners. We had to be very selective with our clothing. I took charge of a large holdall crammed with extras, toiletries,

raincoats and an umbrella. In those days the umbrella went everywhere we went. Mum filled another holdall with Julie's baby clothes. The pram was rather large, despite being like a pushchair. It folded up sideways and collapsed onto the four wheels. It was labelled and secured to travel in the guard's van of the train. Dad took charge of the suitcase and the pram. Mum took charge of Julie and the tickets and I was responsible for the two holdalls and a brown carrier bag containing a few sandwiches and biscuits for the journey. Thus loaded up, we started our journey to Hayling Island by catching the Corporation bus from East Park Road to London Road Station.

The trains were always crowded, so Dad made sure which carriage we were seated in before he ran along the platform to put the pram in the guard's van. There always seemed plenty of time when boarding at Leicester because the train originated from the north and the railwayman had to walk down the track tapping the wheels of the train at intervals with a heavy metal rod. He could tell by the sound whether the wheel was overheated or unsafe.

Frequently on a Saturday during the peak holiday period the trains were packed and it was not unusual to travel all the way to our destination standing in the corridor or taking it in turns to sit on our cases. Mum usually managed to obtain a seat because she held Julie in her arms. The journey to St Pancras Station took about 90 minutes and conversation was lively as the train went clickety click, clickety clack across the rails.

Arrival in London was very exciting but crossing to the Victoria Station on the tube train was out of the question. Extra cash had been saved to pay for the luxury of a ride in a taxi. We joined the long queue outside St Pancras Station and waited until it was our turn to take a cab. The drivers never climbed out of the vehicle to assist us. Dad would place the pushchair, still folded up, into the space beside the driver and then wedge it down with the weight of the cases and holdalls. The driver threaded a thick canvas strap through the handles and around the luggage

*Mum, Dad and Julie outside the chalets at Warners Holiday Camp.
(V. Tedder)*

to secure it to a steel bar on the front dashboard. The
luggage was exposed to the elements as we set off. The
trip across London was fascinating. The driver indicated
places of interest as we bobbed in and out of the traffic. At
Victoria Railway Station the luggage was released from the
intricate strapping while Dad sorted out the fare. We then
made our way to join hundreds of other passengers on
the platforms indicating trains for the south coast. They
were very busy lines, with crowds on their way to
Southsea and the neighbouring seaside resorts. Quite a
number were bound for Portsmouth and the ferry to the
Isle of Wight.

At Portsmouth some passengers made their way to
the pier to catch the ferry boats, while we went the
opposite way to catch the train to Havant. There we
changed to a push and pull train to take us across to
Hayling Island. This train only had a couple of coaches and
ran back and forth several times a day between Havant

and Hayling. The guard on this little train was exceptionally
helpful, assisting with luggage, mailbags, pushchairs and
packages which passengers had entrusted to his keeping in
the guard's van.

The train ran along a single track and at one stage
crossed a low iron bridge over a short stretch of water
and marshland. We actually left the mainland for about a
quarter of a mile. Not many people seemed to visit
Hayling Island at that time. There was one hotel, a few
guest houses, three public houses that took in guests, some
holiday flats and the holiday camp. The rest of the
properties were made up of cottages, beautiful houses and
bungalows. There were a few shops scattered about the
island and a post office. It was a very quiet place.

When we arrived at the little station at West Town we
discovered that we had a short walk to the holiday camp
by taking a footpath through the park. We crossed the
main road and on a side lane was the entrance to
Warners. We were impressed by the cleanliness, good
paintwork and the well cultivated flower gardens. People
had been arriving all day at the camp, but it was after 5pm
when we booked in. Our journey had taken most of the
day.

Everyone in reception was kind and efficient and
within minutes we were allocated our chalet and given a
handful of brochures concerning events taking place during
the week. An instruction booklet informed us of the camp
rules, meal times and other items we needed to know. A
teenage boy, very tanned and cheeky, made us laugh as he
led the way to our chalet with the luggage precariously
balanced on a wooden trolley. Julie's pushchair had been
unfolded and put to use as soon as we arrived at the
station at West Town.

We followed the young lad around the large swimming
pool, across a lawn and flower gardens, to a chalet situated
in the centre of a row of twelve. It was nicely situated, not
too near the ballroom or the pool. The chalets were
painted a bottle green colour with white window frames

and fancy eaves. Everything looked bright and clean. In the centre of the chalet was the door, flanked each side by a curtained window. We walked immediately into a sitting room area with wardrobes and chests of drawers along the sides. Beyond was the small bathroom and the toilet. On the left, through narrow doors, were two bedrooms. Julie and I had the rear room and Mum and Dad the front. Our room overlooked gardens and had two single beds in it. My parents had two single beds, but they were pushed together to make a double. There was little room to move about in, but it was anticipated that the chalet would only be used for sleeping and changing in. The rest of the time we expected to be out and about joining in the social activities. Even in wet weather events were arranged in the ballroom, so there was always somewhere to go and something to see even if we did not join in.

Meals were arranged at set times - 8.30am breakfast, 1pm lunch and 6.30pm dinner. We had heard of the strict regime concerning meals at the Butlins holiday camps, where meals were taken at long tables, and we were pleasantly surprised at the Warners arrangements. We found it a very relaxed atmosphere and folk could wander in for meals within a reasonable time of the bell sounding. Tables were set to accommodate four persons or less. Large tables were available for families of six and above. We all had plenty of room to move about.

Mothers could take their children to another dining area for a special children's meal an hour before the adult mealtimes, so that they could leave their offspring in the care of capable and responsible nursemaids in a playroom while they ate their meal in comfort. However, children were welcome to dine in the main hall with their parents if they so wished, and high chairs were provided. All children were expected to remain seated at the table until their parents had finished the meal, and were then escorted out of the dining room. It all seemed reasonable and there were no complaints. The food was excellent with a varied menu. We ate everything put before us. It was cooked well

and served efficiently by pleasant and cheerful waitresses.

Although there was a daily programme of events we only participated in those that appealed to us. Consequently we were able to take advantage of visits to the beach and walks around the island. The beach was situated about half a mile from the main entrance, so the pushchair, loaded with our beach needs and Julie's bucket and spade, was frequently used for the morning or afternoon session on the sands. Sometimes we did not bother with the pushchair but walked to the sea front to catch a bus to the ferry terminus on the west of the island. It was only a small ferry boat that crossed to Milton for Southsea. At the terminus was a public house, a shop and a small area to park three cars. A special area was marked out so that the bus could turn for the return journey. The beach was wonderful with soft white sand and the sea, gently lapping along the coastline, was a safe place to paddle. The children loved this part of the coast but there was danger in swimming because the currents not far from the shore were strong and easily swept swimmers out to sea. We spent hours on this beach using the old white concrete tank traps half buried in the sand as a back rest. Some of the concrete blocks were piled on top of one another and made good places to change out of wet bathing costumes into dry clothes. The boys had marvellous games playing cowboys and Indians or soldiers in and around them. We had to be extremely alert when changing. It was only a short walk along the beach to take refreshment at the pub or the tiny shop cafe.

Sometimes for a change we put Julie in the pushchair and walked to the east side of the island to the village of Eastoke. We would cross by the path through the sand dunes or follow the road. The village was small, very pretty and had several quaint shops and cafes. The local pub was always busy. Occasionally we were happy just to wander along the traffic free lanes admiring the gorgeous cottages and properties of those fortunate enough to live in such a pleasant place. It was far removed from the smells and

Julie as 'buttercup' at Warners Holiday Camp. (V. Tedder)

noise of Nottingham Road. We vowed to buy a house and live on Hayling Island if we ever won the pools.

Warm summer evenings offered pleasant walks through the back roads and footpaths to the West Town Hotel or The Tudor Rose public house. Either place welcomed and accommodated the visitor. The West Town, rather an up-market establishment, had a large garden and lawns where children could play while the adults had a drink or two relaxing on the cane chairs. The Tudor Rose was an old thatched building and was surrounded by

gardens full of roses. There were old wooden garden seats and tables set out on the lawns that were divided by small rose gardens. The perfume from the flowers, at times, was rather overpowering but a wonderful sight to see. July was obviously the best month to see the roses in full bloom. We gave quite a bit of custom to these establishments, relaxing in the luxury they offered until it was time to walk back to the camp in the dusk and before Julie fell asleep.

We made use of the baby listening service a couple of times, but we always checked on Julie every half an hour. All one had to do to alert the staff that there was a baby sleeping in the chalet, was to tie a large white handkerchief on the door knob. Any child heard crying was reported by the night staff on patrol and the message was given out over the tannoy system in the ballroom. Nursery nurses and the security men who walked around the camp all though the night keeping checks on the property, babies and drunks, although there were very few in those days, were extremely conscientious and no baby cried for long. Most people at the holiday camp were family groups so it was not a problem.

The announcements over the tannoy were very pleasant. The compere would stop the evening proceedings the minute he received a message to say, 'Baby crying in chalet number...'. It was expected that a parent would return to their chalet immediately and they usually did. It was noticeable that many fathers did the honours, leaving the mothers to enjoy the evening undisturbed.

At the end of the evening the entertainment came to a close with the singing of 'Goodnight Campers' to the refrain of 'Goodnight Sweetheart', followed by the National Anthem. Quietly we left the ballroom and bars to stroll back to the chalets. Some youngsters went for midnight swims in the floodlit pool, but if there was any noise whatsoever they were reprimanded by the security patrols who kept a sharp watch on proceedings. Loud noise and shouting was banned and anyone misbehaving in this manner was warned only once. If they persisted, next morning they were asked to leave and were escorted off the premises. Rarely was there any trouble of this nature because the organisers were strict and kept their word. In addition there was always the backing of the family campers. In all the years we went to holiday camps there was only one occasion when we witnessed two young men being escorted off the premises. We later discovered the reason. They had been misbehaving in the bar the previous evening. They had too much to drink and were objectionable to the staff and customers when their requests for more beer were refused.

The organisers of the sporting events appeared to have thought of everything and we were encouraged to participate in the heats, playing against one another in our own time until the finals were reached on the Friday morning. Some enthusiasts, we noticed, took part in so many of the sports that they seemed to be doing nothing else all week. We restricted ourselves to the fun sports like the obstacle, sack, three-legged and egg and spoon races. Julie was encouraged to enter the children's events. Dad and I entered the swimming gala, struggling and roaring with laughter at the antics the compere got up to while we were trying to take the races seriously.

Dad entered the plate collecting competition. Twenty four white enamel plates were skimmed across the pool into the deep end. Each male competitor dived in and retrieved as many plates as possible before coming up for air. Dad did very well. He was under the water such a long time that the audience stood up around the pool edge to see if he was in trouble. We could see him swimming about below, but it seemed a long time before he surfaced again. He received loud applause when he swam to the side, and even more when the plates were counted and he had recovered them all. Mum was rather perturbed by him holding his breath under the water for so long, but she had to admit he did not suffer as a result. No one else reached

Valerie (far left) in the 'topsy turvy' night at Warners Holiday Camp. (V. Tedder)

his standard so on Friday evening in the ballroom he collected his prize, a voucher for one pound which had to be spent in the bar or at the camp shop. My father bought a round of drinks.

The entries of both my sister and I came from a different quarter. Mum and I used our talents to advantage and walked away with the fancy hat and fancy dress competitions. Making use of cardboard, crepe paper and glue purchased from the village shop, we made Julie a paper costume. She represented a buttercup dressed in green and yellow. She looked very pretty and dainty, especially with a little yellow skull cap with a green stalk sticking out of the crown. She was pleased to win first prize of a five shillings voucher and took great delight in spending it on a toy from the camp gift shop.

As for me, I won a prize dressed as Carmen Miranda. I wore a backless bathing costume trimmed with paper frills around the neck and arms. Attached to the waist at the back was a long paper train trimmed with three rows of frills. My legs were exposed at the front. On my tummy, holding the paper together Mum stitched paper flowers and ribbons. My headdress was a paper hat with paper flowers attached. This was sewn to a headscarf and tied tightly around my head. My prize was a one pound voucher. I purchased a small ornament from the gift shop as a souvenir, but it got broken during the journey home.

I came second in the fancy hat competition by making a hat from a paper plate covered with green foliage, leaves and wild flowers and aptly named Woodland View. This time I received a box of chocolates for my trouble. We enjoyed making up the garments sitting outside our chalet for a couple of hours and then receiving the praise from other campers for our ingenuity.

Dad and I won third prizes for dressing up on Topsy Turvy night. This was for adults only, but it was all clean fun and the children were as much involved as their parents. They enjoyed watching the adults making fools of themselves in their outrageous outfits. We borrowed clothes from one another and there was a great sense of fun and friendliness. Offers to lend items of apparel were readily forthcoming and it was no trouble finding someone of similar build to borrow a garment or other. I wore a jacket and a pair of flannels borrowed from a young man I had made friends with and Dad lent me his white shirt and a tie. A neighbour lent me his cap, which was miles too big and had to be stuffed with newspaper to stop it slipping down over my eyes. I then borrowed a walking stick and purchased cotton wool from a local shop to make eyebrows, a moustache and a beard. A pair of spectacles borrowed from Mum finished the transformation. I walked with my shoulders bent over, leaning on the stick. One of the competition rules was that we had to look like a male or female so convincingly that no one guessed who we were. In my case I succeeded but gave the game away by sitting at the same table as my parents for the evening.

Dad on the other hand had difficulties. He was tall and well made and Mother had nothing to fit him. An elderly lady, rather large herself, offered him a dress and a hat.

Another lady lent him a pair of bloomers. By the time Mum had finished with him, by adding makeup and jewellery, he passed off well as a woman, although still a rather large one. He padded out his chest with socks to give him shape and wore stockings held around the knees with elastic and the legs of the bloomers. Unfortunately his feet let him down. No woman had shoes big enough for him. He made do with his own brown sandals. However, when it came to the competition he received a good round of applause and received third prize. There was a lot of skylarking and mickey taking, but there was nothing offensive despite showing off knickers, suspenders and bras. What a laugh we had that night and again next day when we went around handing back the items we had borrowed. And what was Dad's prize? Another voucher.

During the evening, the camp photographer had taken photographs and the following morning they were displayed on a very large noticeboard for all to see. We went into hysterics laughing at the poses some of the men had arranged themselves in an effort to copy females. The photographs were not expensive and we always purchased the ones we were on irrespective of whether they were good or not.

One of the afternoons was set aside for the Donkey Derby. We saw about a dozen well groomed donkeys arrive while we were at lunch. They were driven into the sports field along a path at the rear of the camp and given buckets of water. The course was marked out with white tape attached to stakes driven into the ground, and measured about an eighth of a mile. A square winners' enclosure was set out near to the tables used for the betting. There were six races with five donkeys in each, enabling the donkeys to be interchanged during the afternoon programme. The jockeys were the children, who clamoured for the privilege but had to be between the ages of seven and ten to participate. There was no shortage of volunteers as there had to be different children for each race. The jockeys were given a coloured vest with a number on the back just before the start of each race.

It started very seriously with the inspection of the chosen donkeys for the particular race. Then we queued up to wager a sixpence on the one we fancied to win. The stake money was split between the first, second and third which amounted to quite a few pounds as the Donkey Derby attracted quite a lot of attention and there were not many campers absent. We chose the donkey we thought might win but found that the children were given the freedom to choose which one they wanted to ride. There was no way we could foretell a winner under this system. The children mounted their chosen animal and as soon as the race started half of them were unseated. It was great fun. Some fathers stepped forward and hoisted their child back onto the donkey but all was lost by this time. It was hilarious with nearly all the jockeys sliding off at some stage. One or two donkeys stopped running altogether and a few never even got started.

Eventually, as the evening progressed, we noticed that it was the same two or three donkeys that kept winning. There was nothing we could do as we did not know which child with its numbered vest would ride them. It was an afternoon of hit and miss, laughter and screams of desperation. For a total of three shillings we had a wonderful, hilarious time.

The week went by very quickly and before we knew it we were saying farewell to many friends. Our first venture with holiday camps was declared a great success and we

Mum, Dad and Julie at Corton, 1950
(V. Tedder)

agreed that we had not had so much fun for years. We promised ourselves further visits. In fact, over the next twelve years we had one and two week holidays at several holiday camps, usually Warners, but we also tried Maddisons and Pontins. We returned to Hayling Island . numerous times before varying our destinations, visiting Kent, Burnham-on-Sea, Hemsby and the Isle of Wight.

Our return journey from Bembridge on the Isle of Wight one year was a catastrophe. We arrived on the island all right and enjoyed a marvellous holiday. On the Saturday we were to return home, the crews of the ferries held a strike and were running a skeleton service from Ryde to Portsmouth Harbour. We arrived at Ryde Pier at about 11.30am to catch our particular ferry, only to find the place milling with hundreds of people and stacks of luggage along the pavement outside the pier and in the waiting rooms. At that time the ferry was the only means of public transport to the mainland. We had no option but to wait with everyone else. We had our return tickets and joined the slow moving crowd through the gates towards the pier, with Julie's pushchair loaded with luggage. The long queues wound up and down the pier with the crowd being kept in line by frequent visits from the Harbour Master and his assistants. When the ferries arrived we all moved slowly forward in an orderly fashion until boarding was stopped.

When we left the holiday camp earlier that day the sun was shining, but as the day progressed the skies became overcast and the wind came up very strongly. By the time our turn came to board the ferry at 5pm, we had stood in the queue for several hours not daring to leave it for anything. We took turns in running to the toilet or to get a drink from the cafe. During that period the rain poured in torrents and the wind howled. At one point we thought we might get blown off the pier because it was so strong, but we stood our ground with our backs to the wind and suffered. We were all soaked to the skin in no time. We became extremely cold and huddled together to keep out of the wind and to keep warm. The cafe at the end of the pier did a roaring trade that day with the endless stream of cups of hot drinks and food.

As a result of the long wait for the ferry, it made our train connections late and we eventually arrived home extremely late at night. The following day when we assessed the situation, we had all suffered clothing damage from the foul weather. My plastic raincoat was about an inch and a half shorter than my new summer coat. It was a grey herringbone material with black buttons. Where the rain had continually run down towards the hem there was a dirty mark around the bottom. My new black shoes, purchased especially for the holiday but never worn

because of the good weather, had fitted me perfectly. By the time I had finished squelching about in the inches of water all day they were soaked, stretched far too big for me. Mum and Julie had similar damage and marks to their clothing and shoes. Dad's trousers were never the same again from the knees down. The dry cleaning bill was expensive and the coats and Dad's trousers always carried a faint stain mark.

The suitcase also suffered. It was not leather but a combination of mixed fibres. When we opened it the clothing was soaking wet. The case had stood in the puddles that had become deeper as the day wore on, and had soon lost its shape. Julie and I did not help either by sitting on the case while waiting. The case was bowed and the lid gaped all the way around. It was only the locks that held it together. When it dried out, the lid did not fit properly and so it was difficult to close. That holiday was certainly one to remember.

At all the holiday camps we managed to win prizes for miscellaneous competitions. I remember that Dad won first prize in a Look Alike Competition. The crowd decided he was so much like Lee Marvin that he was nicknamed Lee for the rest of the week. Another time he won the Knobbly Knees Competition. The prizes were always vouchers to be spent at the gift shop or at the bar.

Eventually events changed and we moved onto caravan holidays but the friendships and fun were never the same. I think the days spent at the camps were some of the best we ever had in our lives and we still have a great many photographs to prove it.

The family at Warners Holiday Camp, Hayling Island, 1951 (V. Tedder)

A present from 'Down Under'

My Australian penfriend, Margot Anderson. (V. Tedder)

Just before my 16th birthday I received a present from Australia. It was my first pair of nylon stockings. They were wonderful, so fine and cobweb thin. They could not be bought in Leicester shops. As I removed them from their tissue paper and cellophane wrapping, I was amazed by the delicate hosiery. It was practically transparent and down the back seam was worked a rope design. The stockings were a dark brown shade with reinforced toes and heels. Above the heel was a fancy picture frame pattern about three inches in length which tapered off into a narrow point, and the stockings were fashioned into a leg shape. I cried with excitement and joy to be in possession of such a prize. No one could have given me a more wonderful gift. To have such items readily on sale in Australia was beyond comprehension. I felt we were sadly lacking in fashion in this country and wondered how long it would be before such beautiful fine stockings were on sale in our shops. We were still having to put up with lisle stockings. Now I understood why the young girls and women went mad on stockings given to them by the American servicemen while they were over here during the war.

How did it come about for me to receive such a present? Well, it all began several years earlier during the Second World War.

My dad served in the Pacific during the hostilities and his ship made a couple of visits to Australia for refits and provisions. Sometime during 1944, while in port at Perth, along with other members of the ship's company he was invited by Australian families to take shore leave at their homes and on their farms. My dad stayed with a family named Anderson who owned a large sheep farm outside Perth. He was well looked after and fascinated by the vastness of the land owned by his host. The Andersons had a daughter named Margot who was about the same age as me and eager to start correspondence with an English pen pal, so Dad put her in touch with me. From then on, we became pen pals. I was just as eager to write back and we wrote good newsy letters. In the beginning our letters crossed the world two or three times a year. Letters took a long time by the sea route as we often could not afford the extra price for airmail. By the time we were teenagers correspondence had increased to sending and receiving seven or eight letters a year. I sent her small gifts at Christmas and on birthdays. In return I received a number of books about Australian flora and fauna, handkerchiefs embroidered with the most famous of Australian flowers and other linen. One Christmas I received six silver dessert spoons and the following year six silver dessert forks to match. Through our letters we exchanged knowledge of our countries and we often said how much we would like to meet one day.

Margot stayed on at school longer than me because she wanted to be a nurse. The standard and need for the right qualifications was always mentioned in her letters. There was a suggestion that she might come over to visit us and do some training at the Leicester Royal Infirmary. It appears that this hospital had a reputation in Australia for good nurse training. We offered to accommodate her if she decided to come over, but what she would have thought about our house and our standard of living compared to hers did not bear thinking about. However, as it happened, she never came.

She sent me photographs of herself and her friends in

their nurses uniforms and they looked a fine body of young women. Margot was dark haired, with a round happy face and most attractive.

There was a time after the war when Dad wanted to take up the offer of emigrating to Australia to work on the sheep farm. The Australian government encouraged emigrants where families had a sponsor. We had the Andersons ready to take charge and look after our welfare until we were established. The passage was paid by the Australian government and all we had to do was pay a deposit of ten pounds each. The fare was paid back after we were in employment and settled. After months of correspondence a letter finally arrived setting out what was on offer for us and a plea to take it up. They had agreed to act as our sponsors. They had a large caravan on their land for us to live in until a house was acquired or built. Dad had a job waiting for him on the sheep farm and I had a job waiting for me at the local post office when I reached school leaving age. Mum, because Julie was still a baby, would have to assist the other female members of the family in the domestic chores of the farm and the cooking for the farm labourers. It all sounded most exciting. It was estimated that we would probably be about two years getting established, then Dad could move on if he wanted to work at something else. It all appeared very satisfactory and I wanted to be part of this great adventure. Dad was very much for going, and although I did not have any say in the matter I agreed to pull my weight if we did. Mum would not agree. She was not prepared to put up with the hardship it entailed until a proper house was available. Neither did she feel she wanted to be part of the domestic scene. She had too many family ties but agreed to consider every possibility of emigrating before giving her final decision. I heard Mum and Dad discussing it at night while I was in bed and knew then we should not be going. After a few weeks Mum finally said no. Dad set about writing a suitable letter to the Andersons declining their most generous offers and apologising for any inconvenience entailed. Over the years Mum often said she was glad we had not emigrated. Dad never said very much. I always felt he would have welcomed a new start after the war as he was very impressed with what he saw on his visits to Perth. He loved the city and stated what a wonderful and beautiful place it was. In addition there was the glorious sunny weather.

As the years progressed and the living situation at Nottingham Road became worse with all we had to endure from the dye works and the sooty chimney, I often declared that I thought we would have fared better in Australia. After all, our move to Nottingham Road and Dad's job as the boilerman for the dye works was nothing to shout about. However we did not go and that was that. The Andersons were very understanding and continued to write to my parents.

Margot and I corresponded for many years, from 1944 to 1958. Eventually she married and moved to Melbourne. I changed my career and letters to one another became fewer. One day I realised we had not written to each other for nearly two years. When I did write it was too late. She had moved on and there was no reply from the family. After fourteen years it ended. Perhaps one day we shall contact each other again. There would be so much to tell from both sides of the world.

As for the nylon stockings they were Sunday best and worn only on special occasions. No one touched them but me. When I had hand washed them, I wrapped them carefully in a tea towel to pat out the excess moisture before hanging them to dry over another smooth tea towel on the clothes horse. They never went outside in the wind to dry. They lasted nearly two years. Eventually I had several drawn threads and a neatly repaired hole in the toe, but I was so careful I wanted them to last forever. Unfortunately I went to a Christmas party at the church schoolroom and was involved in a game of musical chairs. As I turned the corner sharply to plonk myself down on a chair as the music stopped, I slipped down onto my knees and slithered along the inlaid wooden floor. Both knees were scraped and bleeding and my precious nylons ruined. I remember sitting on the floor rubbing and hugging my knees and crying. Everyone thought it was because I had hurt myself but it was for my cut and laddered stockings. They were totally ruined and had to be thrown away. It broke my heart at the time.

It was about this time that I had another catastrophe. We had been invited to join my mother's sister Edie and her husband Harold at their holiday chalet at Corton near Great Yarmouth for a few days in August. I needed a bathing costume. I decided it would be cheaper to knit one and found a very smart looking costume pattern. The wool suggested was double knitting wool and the pattern was like a basket weave. Quickly I set about knitting it in a bottle green colour. It did not take me long. After a week or so of constant knitting every spare minute, I proudly produced a nicely fitted garment. I could not wait to wear it and try it out in the sea. We struck lucky with the weather having glorious sunshine everyday. As soon as possible I donned the costume and ran into the sea. The North Sea is always cold at the best of times, even in the hottest of weather, but I braved the cool temperature and enjoyed my swim. When I came out of the water the costume had stretched beyond belief. The water had caused it to go completely out of shape. It looked atrocious. The costume hung down at the bottom and between my legs with the weight of the water. The straps had stretched and the bust part sagged. It was terrible and I felt quite embarrassed as I crossed the crowded beach. Mum said I was not to worry. When the water drained out of it and it dried it would be alright. I did not need it dry, I needed to wear it when wet. I felt terrible and upset. All my hard work for nothing. The moral of this little story is never wear a hand-knitted bathing costume if you intend to get it wet. Needless to say, I saved my pocket money and purchased a proper stylish costume from Marks and Spencer's store. I learned that cheapness does not always pay.

The family with Aunt Edie and Uncle Harold on Corton beach, near Great Yarmouth, 1948. (V. Tedder)
Below: Valerie wearing her knitted bathing costume, with the family. (V. Tedder)

Stagestruck

I was a typical teenager, interested in all the new films, British and American, that were on the circuit. Too young, in my mother's eyes, to go out dancing, I was restricted to the social activities offered at the church. I needed something more adult to broaden and satisfy my leisure time. The cinema seemed to be the answer and my parents did not object so long as I saw suitable films. I was allowed to go once a week in the city and twice if one visit was to a local cinema, the Evington, Trocadero or the Shaftesbury.

I became quite a fan, saving my pocket money to see my favourite stars. Sometimes I went to the cinema accompanied by a girl friend at work, but it was usually alone. Going straight from work at 6pm, I arrived in the city centre in about half an hour. There was always a good choice of cinemas within easy walking distance of the bus stop. I managed to attend them all in turn.

The Gaumont in the Market Place was my favourite. To enter the cinema we were shown by the usherettes along a brightly lit staircase and through a door situated at the side. The place seemed enormous with the rows of seats stretching across the auditorium and up an incline to the back. Above was the balcony stretching the width of the cinema. Long, gold coloured curtains covered the screen in a semicircle above the stage.

· Then there was the Odeon in Queen Street, a more conventional cinema which was entered from the back and equally as big as the Gaumont. Both were often full to capacity. Often when entering the Odeon cinema we were distracted by the film as we fumbled and stumbled our way through the rows of seats, completely ignoring the flashing torch light that was being shone on a seat half way along a row by the usherette and her hushed voice hurrying us along.

The Picture House, in Granby Street, made me feel slightly peculiar when entering from the large open foyer.

Leicester Market Place and Gaumont Cinema, 1957. (Leicester City Council)

The door was next to the screen which made the film seem enormous and look as if it was about to wrap itself around you. As one walked along the aisle up a slight incline to the seats, the screen behind appeared to shrink to normal size. In this cinema I always walked two thirds of the way in before finding a seat. Unfortunately we were often distracted from the screen because each time the door was opened to admit a patron, the daylight flashed through for a few seconds.

My visits to the cinema were often spoilt because I always went straight in. The programmes were continuous and, without fail, I saw the last half hour of the main feature film first. This was because I had to leave the cinema about half an hour before the end to catch the last bus home. So, frequently, I knew who had done it, or whether the film had a happy ending or not, before the story unfolded.

If the films were popular and had been given good reviews in the newspapers I queued to get in. An odd seat was usually available. On these occasions I saw the film from start to finish. I had a system of calculating how many minutes I had after the film finished to reach the bus stop. Towards the end of the film I would leave my seat and stand at the back near to the exit, watching the last few scenes. I was not the only one as many people did the same. There was no time to watch the credits or stand for the National Anthem. I would be heading for the door as the last scene flashed onto the screen. Then it was a mad dash to catch the bus. My parents accepted no excuses if I was late home. Of course, there were some occasions when despite my effort to catch the bus I would see it pulling away from the stop. No time to stop and swear, I ran all the way home. Being young and healthy, I usually managed to get home as quickly as the bus journey took, and breathlessly entered the house more or less on time.

Another cinema frequently visited was the Cameo in High Street. This was a very old cinema which concentrated on showing many silent films and Walt Disney cartoons. I remember seeing Pearl White tied to the railway lines as an express train rushed towards her, and Mary Pickford beseeching her lover not to leave her with much thumping of the breast and outstretched hands. There was a run of comedy films starring Charlie Chaplin, Laurel and Hardy, Bud Abbot and Lou Costello, and the Keystone Cops. The range of films was changed once a fortnight and there was always a good selection at each performance. The shows lasted for about an hour and a half.

My parents, Julie and I went to see these shows regularly. It was suitable for Julie and we all laughed at the antics of Tom and Jerry, Daffy Duck and Tweetie Pie. Sometimes the performances included a serial, Flash Gordon, a space story, or a cowboy film and it always included the latest Pathe Newsreel report.

I saw a lot of films over the years and I accumulated my fair share of heart-throbs. Over our machines at work we were allowed to have pin-up photographs. One I had was James Dean. The others changed periodically as I transferred my hero worship from one star to another. Whenever we had been to see a film, the following day was spent telling everyone about it, except for the ending. We were quite loyal to one another by keeping the thrilling part, or the person who had done it, a secret. This exchange of film news kept us up to date and gave us some idea whether the film was worth seeing or not. The cinema magazine cost about one shilling and sixpence so we took it in turns to buy one and then hand it round at work.

Whether going regularly to the cinema so much affected me I cannot say, but there was an occasion when I became so star-struck that I replied to an advertisement in the *Leicester Mercury* when a certain producer was looking for persons to take part in an amateur production of the musical 'Gypsy'. The show was to be performed on four evenings during December at the Brice Memorial Hall on Queens Road, Leicester. The advertisement stated that singers were required for leading roles, the chorus and persons with various skills for backstage scenes. I could sing, having performed solos at many church services, and could sew. Both I thought would be acceptable and it might be fun.

Mum was dubious when I told her of my new venture but said that as long as there was no expense involved she did not see why I could not go along to the audition. I went along on the appropriate evening and took my place in the queue of budding starlets, having filled in a form to state what I could do and any experience I had. Then we had to sing a few bars from any song we knew and read several lines from the proposed show. About half an hour later, the list of persons accepted plus a list of reserves was read out loud. I was in luck. I had been chosen for the chorus and had a two line part to learn. No dancing was involved as a special troupe had been engaged for that task. All the chorus had to do was to sway and move their arms in time to the music. I thought it was marvellous and immediately set about learning my role. The following few months were exciting as I attended the hall twice a week for the rehearsals. It was very interesting, a look behind the scenes and I looked forward to the actual performances. In the meantime we were instructed on the type of costumes to be worn. My role involved wearing a long evening dress,

Theatre Royal, Horsefair Street, Leicester. (Leicester City Council)

long elbow length gloves, silver or gold shoes and plenty of bright jewellery. The chorus part required a gypsy costume. In both cases the main costume was provided. Finding and borrowing the accessories from friends and relatives was easy.

I thoroughly enjoyed the performances played before a packed hall each evening. On the last night, a Saturday evening, we were treated to tea or coffee and cake after the performance, accompanied by a speech of thanks from the producer and a plea to keep in touch for another musical the following year. The 'do' after the performance made me late leaving the premises. I had two buses to catch home. When I realised the time, I grabbed the bag containing my borrowed bits and pieces and ran all the way to the bus stop, just managing to catch it as it drew away from the stop. It was the last one along Queens Road. Arriving at Victoria Park gates, I was too late to catch the next one to East Park Road. Well, I had missed buses before and thought nothing of running all the way home. I was very excited about the show and the success and was eager to tell my parents about it. Also, I was one of those chosen to make contact with the producer the following year. When I got to the back door, I did not get a word in. Mum took one look at me and lost her temper. First, I was

chastised for being late home and secondly, she objected to the make-up I was wearing. She said I looked like a painted doll and a common slut, a woman of the streets and it was a wonder I was not accosted on the way home. The fact that I had travelled on a bus with such heavy make-up on was a disgrace. What had happened was that in my excitement of the occasion and having to make a dash for the last bus, I had completely forgotten to wash off the stage make-up. The success of the venture lost its lustre and I went to bed with a well scrubbed face and a few tears. I was very upset and did not mention the musical again. Overnight I lost interest and made no attempt to take part in any further amateur dramatics. The four excellent and enjoyable performances of 'Gypsy' were my first and last venture into the world of theatre. From then on, I watched from the auditorium.

At sixteen, I had a chance of going away on holiday with a friend. We attended the same church, although Audrey was far more religious than me, as were her parents. We seemed to get along well together and enjoyed going to the cinema, theatre and the church socials. She was a year older than I and a secretary. I was amazed at the speed at which she could write shorthand. She was an only child and I suppose she thought that my company would be good on holiday. Her parents had agreed and it was up to my parents whether I went or not. I was all for it. Audrey and I put our heads together and planned to go off exploring, leaving her parents to take a more sedate and quieter holiday.

The chosen resort was Ilfracombe, a place I had not visited before. I was shown brochures and it looked a pleasant and exciting place. My parents, after much discussion, making sure that I really wanted to go and that I was able to save enough money to pay board, train fare and pocket money, finally gave their permission.

The arrangements were that we would travel by train overnight to Exeter then change to another train to Ilfracombe. We were to stay at a guest house, rooms only, because the landlady would prepare and cook all our meals from what we purchased daily. I thought it a peculiar arrangement but that was the system adopted by many holiday establishments at that time.

On the Friday evening of departure and the beginning of the August bank holiday week, I went along to my friend's home with a packed suitcase and a small holdall of necessities that I would need for the overnight journey. We left Audrey's house in time to make the journey by local bus to the L.M.S. railway station on London Road. Our train was to depart about 10.30pm. When we arrived at the station, the booking hall and the car park were crowded with holiday-makers waiting for the overnight trains to the coastal resorts. Large placards indicated where the queues were to form for places like Blackpool, Great Yarmouth, Skegness, London, Southsea and Exeter. It seemed as if the whole of Leicester work force was going on holiday. The station waiting rooms, cafes and platforms were packed to capacity and everyone seemed happy and in a holiday mood. The *Leicester Mercury* had taken photographs of the crowds at the station on previous years and now I was seeing it first hand. It was fascinating to watch small groups of people gradually increase in number as members of their families arrived. In some cases there were as many as ten or twelve in a family, all going to the same resort together.

Audrey's father located the correct place for us to queue prior to our being allowed down onto the platform. When our train arrived there was such a scurrying as we climbed aboard and found our reserved seats. It was exciting. I had travelled extensively in my young life but never overnight. This was something new and thrilling. Soon every seat was occupied. Luggage racks above our heads were weighted down with suitcases, bags and coats. In between the seats rested smaller bags, which later were taken out and opened to reveal flasks of tea, bottles of lemonade and sandwiches, to be consumed during the long journey. A whistle blew, the guard waved a green flag

and slowly the train drew out of the station. A cheer went up in the carriage and 'We're off. Lookout seaside, here we come,' was shouted by several enthusiastic holidaymakers.

As I remember we were due to arrive at Exeter about 4am, and change to another train to arrive at Ilfracombe by 8am. The journey was pleasant and it was lovely to see the lights of the villages and towns as we sped through the night. I watched in wonder as the dawn came up and made sense of the shapes on the landscape. Soon the rhythmic sound of the clickety click of the wheels as they crossed the joints made us drowsy and we nodded off to sleep.

We were not to book into the guest house before 10am so we had no option but to sit and wait on the promenade. We carried our luggage to the sea front, found a suitable seat and sat admiring the view until it was time to move on. The guest house was situated near to the sea front and was pleasant and clean. The landlady made us welcome and although she was polite, I could tell she was going to be strict as she laid down the house rules within minutes of our arrival.

Audrey and I shared a twin bedded room, with her parents in a double room next door. We all shared the same bathroom and had to give notice when we required a bath. We had sole use of the front lounge and dining room and everything we needed, except food, was provided.

Breakfast was fixed at 8.30am and dinner at 6.30pm. Whatever we needed to eat we bought and the landlady cooked it. I thought it a daft arrangement but, apart from being asked what I liked and disliked, it was not my problem.

I recall the weather was very kind to us with many long sunny days. Audrey and I went swimming a couple of times at the local baths but we never wore our bathing costumes on the beach. Although I had been swimming in the sea before and loved it, I felt that Audrey's parents did not approve and I did not suggest it. In fact, during conversation one afternoon, I said how lovely it would be to go into the sea and I was told by her parents that I could if I wished, but it was obvious they disapproved.

We attended the local church on the Sunday and went for several walks. Much to my disappointment, Audrey and I were not allowed to go exploring by ourselves. We were chaperoned all the time. Daily we held a conference on what we would be eating that night for dinner and where we would spend the day. First we went shopping and took back the food to the landlady. Then it was out for the day. We were not encouraged to return to the guest house during the day and not before 6pm.

Ilfracombe was a nice place and very crowded. There was plenty to see and do. We went on several coach trips to visit smaller places like Hele, Combe Martin and Bay and Woolacombe Bay. I remember Woolacombe Bay was ideal for surfing. Whatever we did or wherever we went, we had to be back at the guest house in time for the evening meal at 6.30pm which was prepared and always on time. Afterwards most evenings we strolled along the front, listened to the band and then returned to the guest house for tea or coffee and biscuits at 9.30pm. There was no television but we were allowed to listen to the small radio provided, or read books and magazines until bedtime.

One evening we booked to see a show at the Winter Gardens, which started at 7.30pm. Consequently, we altered dinner to 6pm then dashed to get to the theatre on time. We were given a key to the front door on this particular occasion because we were to be late back, after 10pm. It was frowned upon if guests stayed out after that time unless going to a show. Ringing the bell for admittance just was not done.

During the holiday I ate too much fruit and ice cream and became covered in heat bumps. Audrey's mother insisted I cover the spots with Calamine lotion which I hated and I walked about looking a sight, smothered in pale pink patches. She dosed me with *Milk of Magnesia*

until I rebelled. Then somebody had trouble going to the toilet and Audrey and I were sent to purchase sennapods from the nearest chemist.

Oh dear, the holiday had started well but it was not what I was used to. Indeed, it was not at all what I expected. Audrey's parents kept their word to my parents that they would keep their eye on me, but they took that responsibility too far. Audrey and I were very restricted in our movements and were chaperoned when we took part in any leisure activities. Even a round of crazy golf was played under the watchful eyes of her parents sitting on a seat nearby. We were fun loving, healthy teenagers but we made no friends and were kept to our two selves. I fell in with all their arrangements and although I enjoyed it to a certain extent and have had many a laugh since, I was glad to get home. I must have been a very well behaved young lady because I was asked to go with them again the following year, but I had other plans. Although Audrey and I remained friends and continued to go out to the cinema, theatre and church socials, her life was totally different to mine and it took a holiday to show just how different. However, I was thankful to her parents for introducing me to the theatre.

Audrey was to celebrate her 18th birthday and, to mark this occasion, her parents treated us to a seat in the dress circle at the Theatre Royal in Horsefair Street, Leicester. It was an evening performance and I looked forward to seeing the play. Going to the theatre was considered by me to be something only the well-to-do could afford and I felt privileged to have been chosen.

The theatre, which I had passed many times and often wondered about, was very impressive from the outside. I thought it resembled a Greek temple, with the four stone pillars at the front rising upwards towards the triangular pediment. Beneath the pillars and covering the pavement to the kerb, was the walkway and entrance to the foyer. It looked quite Victorian in decoration with lots of gold and fancy lampshades.

The evening on which we went was a full house and our reserved seats were excellent, situated opposite centre stage. The play was a comedy called 'Clutterbuck' and although I recall the name of the production and that we constantly laughed at the domestic situations, the actual plot evades my memory. It was a successful evening and it encouraged me to take more interest in the theatre and to make several visits a year in the future.

I remember once leaving work at 6pm and rushing into town to see a special film at the Odeon cinema. After queuing for about half an hour to get in, the commissionaire, in his blue and gold uniform, walked along the queue and stopped opposite a young couple just in front of me. He raised his arm and stated that all those beyond, including me, stood no chance of seeing the performance that night. What a disappointment. There were about twenty behind me in the queue and they all began moaning, but there was nothing to be done about it as the cinema was full to capacity. Slowly making my way back towards the city centre to catch the bus back home, being too late to look for another film, I remembered the Theatre Royal was showing a murder play and hurried along to the theatre hoping to obtain a seat in the upper circle before it started at 7.30pm.

I was lucky to get a seat in the gallery, a part of the theatre I had not been to before. Clasping my ticket, I followed the signs and began to climb the stairs, up, up and up I went until I was out of breath. An usherette checked my ticket at the door at the top and when she opened the door I gasped. The seating was so steep. She indicated my seat, an odd one about a third of the way in from the aisle and on the second row from the front. Precariously I descended the steep steps until I reached the appropriate row, then shuffled and fumbled my way along, excusing myself to other patrons as I went. There was nothing to hold on to and keeping one's balance was essential. The back of the seats of the row in front, which usually was held as a handrail in other theatres or cinemas, was far too

Valerie and Audrey, Ilfracombe, August 1950 (V. Tedder)

low to grasp and seemed to emphasise the steepness of the seating more than ever. Quickly locating my seat and dropping it down, I flopped gratefully onto it just as the lights were being lowered and the small orchestra played the overture.

Despite being afraid to move, I sat glued to the seat and watched a sparkling performance of a thrilling play. The title eludes me but I recall seeing and hearing everything. It was a fantastic seat despite it appearing that I was viewing the performance from the roof. What an experience, and the one and only seat of that type in my life.

I made several visits to the Palace of Varieties near the Haymarket and saw several well known artists performing before packed houses. Then, with the coming of television, the audiences gradually dropped and when the Palace introduced nude shows to attract custom, I decided this was not for me and ceased visiting.

I have many happy memories of the Opera House in Silver Street, mainly because it was the place to see the pantomime each year. My parents took me, and then Julie when she was old enough, most years to see these fine shows. I remember the impressiveness of the theatre, the ornate decoration and paintings on the wall from the foyer to the auditorium. It was always packed in the pantomime season and often we went home a little hoarse from shouting at the baddie or joining in the community singing.

There was one pantomime where a man did a miming act. He danced to a 'Paul Jones'. The stage was totally blacked out except for the spotlight on this brilliant artist. Our imagination was thoroughly engaged as we watched in silence as he danced alone on the stage, first in an imaginary circle holding hands with an invisible partner, then, when the music stopped, he danced with the imaginary partner opposite him, being fat, thin, tall, small, limping, bobbing or taking large or tiny steps. He was hilarious and we shrieked with laughter at his antics. Eventually we laughed until we cried and our sides ached. He received a standing ovation at the completion of his

act. To my shame I never noticed his name and always regretted it. He was indeed an artist of perfection, exceptionally funny and extremely skilled in the art of mime.

CHAPTER FIVE

Spring-cleaning

Always on the lookout for the opportunity to earn extra cash, I was overjoyed when our neighbour Mrs Jackson asked Mum if I would help her with spring-cleaning her house. She would pay for each room as it was completed and for any extra jobs or errands. Mrs Jackson was in her seventies at the time and looked it. She was frail and certain household chores were beyond her capabilities. I think she had a soft spot for me but she was very sharp tongued. She nagged her husband and it was more than his life was worth to be late coming home for his meals or from the allotment.

The spring-cleaning consisted of washing down the paintwork, assisting with the removal and replacement of the net and fabric curtains, dusting furniture, pictures and ornaments and washing and polishing lino floors. There were several small carpet squares to be beaten over the line under the gateway. It did not matter how long it was to take, but each room was to be completed before starting on the next. For this service she offered to pay two shillings and sixpence a room. In addition there would be florins and half crowns for extra work and special errands. I agreed it was a fair price.

Well, under her supervision I set to work during the evenings and Saturday mornings when I was not required to work overtime at the factory. It was extremely hard work on top of a full ten hours with my head bent over a sewing machine, but I persevered and after about eight weeks we had gone right through the house. She paid me when each room was finished as promised. Altogether, with errands and other jobs, I earned one pound ten shillings. With this great sum of money I had saved, I went into Leicester and purchased a pair of navy blue shoes and, with

(R. Pochin & Son Ltd)

the change, treated myself to the cinema.

Mrs Jackson held her washday every Monday morning without fail. She had a large black iron open range in her kitchen and she boiled all her washing in a large aluminium tub on the top. When she was satisfied that it was clean, she removed it from the tub with a pair of hinged copper tongs into a bucket and carried it across the kitchen to a large wooden mangle. The mangle looked enormous to me. It was of black wrought iron, standing on four ornate legs and feet. On the top was a large flat wheel which was turned to tighten or slacken the two wooden rollers as required. In contrast was the small wooden handle attached to the large turning wheel at the side. This too was made of wrought iron, with the name of the manufacturer fashioned in the design around the centre spindle. There was no way could you turn the wheel with one hand and a flick of the wrist. This one was a two-handed job with the arms fully extended, in, up and down in a wide circle. There was space beneath the rollers for a bucket to catch the water.

Mrs Jackson managed to put most of her laundry through the mangle, but there were occasions when she washed large items such as blankets and she called upon her husband to assist.

Mr Jackson worked at John Mason's wood yard further down the street. It was a family concern on Mrs Jackson's side of the family, and he was allowed to return home mid morning and afternoon for his tea breaks. On particularly heavy washdays, Mrs Jackson would wait for her husband, Jim, to come for his morning break and then set him on turning the mangle while she fed the heavy wet items through the rollers. It was very hard work but it certainly squeezed out the majority of water. Together they would hang out the laundry on the two washing lines he had rigged up under the gateway. Invariably Mr Jackson stood up to drink his tea then had to run back to work because his break was over. Poor Mr Jackson, he was very much henpecked. The story of their marriage was sad to a certain extent. They had four sons but the eldest was born prior to the marriage. One day a neighbour told us that Mrs Jackson became pregnant by her true love, but he left her. It was such a disgrace to be pregnant and unmarried that her family sought a husband for her. However, the baby was born before a suitable man was found. Mr Jackson was a young man known to the family who at the time was preparing to emigrate with his two sisters to America. We were told that her family made it worth his while to stay and marry her, which he did. They both appeared to have paid for their mistake one way or another.

I met his sisters when they came over for a visit. They were quite wealthy women and lived in Philadelphia. They were in their sixties and most attractive. After many years in the States they had become very American. One of the sisters told my mum that they had tried numerous times to get Mr Jackson to go and live with them or even visit them, but he always declined. Mrs Jackson did not wish to go. Being a good responsible husband and father, he accepted his obligations and stayed. I saw a sepia photograph of Mrs Jackson when she was quite young. She was a good looker and quite slim, but she seemed to have a stern expression on her face which stayed with her. I always felt it was unwise to cross her. She appeared to have the upper hand when it came to making decisions and Mr Jackson never seemed to argue or disagree with her.

In all the years we knew them, Mrs Jackson was never referred to by Christian name. I think it was Frances but she was always called Mrs Jackson, Mother or Mam, even by her husband and family. On the other hand she frequently referred to Mr Jackson as Dad, Father or Jim. None of us, including my father, called them anything other than Mr and Mrs Jackson.

Mr Jackson was to my mind a typical grandfather type. He was polite, sweet tempered and very pleasant to Julie and me. When he came home for his tea breaks he wore his dirty cream coloured apron with a large front pocket. The apron was tied around his waist by tapes crossed at the back and tied in the front in a bow. His waistcoat just covered the top of the apron at the front. At lunchtimes he came home in his jacket minus the apron. I never discovered what sort of work he did but I believe he was an experienced carpenter and had made numerous pieces of fine furniture in his younger days. Over the Jackson's kitchen, on the flat roof, he had built a greenhouse and he grew tomatoes in large pots. In the summer evenings after having his tea he would climb up a step ladder across the low coal-house roof and up to the roof in order to water and tend his plants. He had rigged up a hosepipe from the kitchen to the greenhouse to save carrying water. On the roof, with no other buildings to obstruct the glass, the fruit grew well and soon ripened. He often supplied us with fresh tomatoes.

As neighbours we got on well together. When they were not well Mum and Dad did their share of keeping an eye on them. There was an occasion during an extremely cold spell one winter when they both took to their bed, suffering from heavy colds and bronchitis. The family paid daily visits but asked my parents to check on them before retiring to bed. Mrs Jackson asked Mum if she would make them a cup of hot Oxo and take it in to them at bedtime. Mum did this every night for about ten days until they were up and about again.

Then came the day when Mr Jackson knocked on the back door. He was upset because he was unable to waken Mrs Jackson. Mum went in and found her in bed. She appeared to be in a coma. The doctor was summoned and he said that he thought she had had a stroke and would not recover. She died a short time later. I had not given much thought about seeing a dead body, especially someone who was not a relative. Mr Jackson invited us into his house to see Mrs Jackson in her coffin before the funeral took place. I did not want to go, but Mum said it was our duty to respect his wishes.

On the day of the funeral and before the relatives arrived, I dutifully followed my mother into his house. In a dimly lit room with the curtains closed, I saw Mrs Jackson lying in state, her coffin balanced on trestles in front of the fireplace. She looked exceedingly small, having shrunk in stature. Her white hair shone and was plaited to one side. Her face seemed to have lost its hardness and the deep character lines were noticeable by their absence. She looked very peaceful but with a yellowish, waxy colour that I have never forgotten. It was a shock to my system seeing her dead body laid out, but she was not my first.

My first was Grandma Howgill who had a stroke on 20 March 1946. It was her 60th birthday and she died a few days later without recovering consciousness. That was a shock to us all and most unexpected.

Being 11 at the time, I was a little afraid of seeing her in her coffin when Mum suggested it but, as Mum said, she had never done me any harm when she was alive so would not harm me now she was dead. I accepted her reasoning but it did not entirely satisfy me. Too young to make any objections and holding Mum's hand for moral support, I went with her into the front room at Kate Street where Gran was lying in state. I recall how cold the room appeared when we entered. Gran looked beautiful. She was dressed in white lace and satin and wore shiny white stockings. Around her neck was a lovely pendant, silver with amethyst stones and a large stone set in the centre. The pendant was resting on a small purple pad on her chest. It was a gift for her birthday from her youngest son, Frank, a soldier serving as a military policeman in India at the time. It was thought fitting that she should wear his gift and be buried with it. I recall how lovely and serene her face was. After seeing her I was no longer afraid of seeing a dead body in a coffin.

I, with several of my cousins and young Julie, did not attend her funeral. We were considered too young. Mother told us later that the hearse and two following cars were covered with wreaths and flowers from relatives, friends, neighbours and customers, past and present. Respect for her was so great that the funeral director, in his morning suit and wearing a top hat with black ribbons flowing from the crown, walked slowly in front of the cortege as it moved along King Richard's Road to St Paul's Church, where the service was to be held and which was packed to capacity. It must have been quite a sight and, when I was older and understood more about death and funerals, I felt sad to have missed being part of it.

Mrs Jackson's funeral was small and simple. Afterwards her husband stayed on alone at the house. He lived a very lonely existence, but his sons and their wives visited and looked after him until he died a few years later.

Factory outings

I was very happy with my employment at the Trafford. I had made a good move and the forelady appeared to take me under her wing. Within a short period of time I was given the opportunity to branch out and learn a further couple of trades. The first was overlocking. Quickly I learned the skill of making up jumpers, sweaters and cardigans, and found it a bonus when we were short of work in the dress and suit department between seasons. I was able to adapt and move over to the overlocking machine for a few weeks, keeping my wages on an even keel.

Secondly, I was encouraged to learn pin tucking. This became fashionable on the collars, pockets and down the fronts of garments, and we had so much work that we performed overtime every night for weeks. The forelady asked me to learn pin tucking to help out with the orders. I found it a very skilled job because it was so easy to stretch the material between the rows. However, there was little variety and I became bored with machining row after row of tiny tucks. On these occasions I was placed on the firm's time, so it did not matter how long it took me to complete a piece of work.

It was during one of these pin tucking sessions that I heard talk of the firm's annual day outing. It was explained to me that the firm hired coaches and arranged a day out, always on a Saturday, at their expense, as a thank you to the workforce for their loyalty and hard work over the previous twelve months. The destination was changed each year and usually the whole of the factory went. All that was needed was to purchase our own food and take some pocket money. I was told that there was no need to have a list of those wanting to go. On the contrary, the firm was well aware of how many employees there were, so only if you did not wish to go for some reason, was it your responsibility to inform the office so that the numbers

could be amended. As far as I recall, everybody went because it was such a fun day out.

It all sounded very exciting and I looked forward to my first factory outing, a day out to Skegness. Of course I had to obtain permission from my parents and, when they were satisfied they knew everything there was to know about it, I was allowed to go.

When the great day arrived, we congregated outside the factory in Lancaster Street at about 6.45am to await the coaches. When they arrived the coaches parked one behind the other all the way along the road. When we were given the signal to board we climbed onto the nearest coach, in company with our friends. Each coach had a supervisor who checked we were all there, then promptly at 7am we were away. We left in convoy for the seaside, stopping for about half an hour en-route for the use of the toilets and some refreshment. It took about four hours along the narrow and winding roads but, just after 11am, we pulled up along the seafront and vacated the coaches. We were to meet in the same spot at 7pm to catch the coaches back home.

I don't remember what we did with ourselves that day. It was fine and windy but we made the best of it doing exactly what we pleased. We had many laughs and purchased silly 'Kiss me quick' hats. The fairground was a big attraction and we spent a couple of hours there trying to win something or other on the darts and shooting ranges. A couple of the young girls made themselves sick by having too many rides on a whiplash merry go round. I recall I was glad I was not tempted to join them.

Everybody turned up for the coaches at 7pm and, when the checking was completed to ensure no one had been left behind, the coaches set off back to Leicester. Halfway home the coaches separated, each one taking a different route to a selected public house so that we could all have a drink. We stopped for one hour, and as I did not drink in pubs a girlfriend and I walked around the village, purchased some chips and a drink from the local fish and chip shop, and returned to wait for the others in the coach. Later as we drove towards Leicester the coaches caught up with each other and we all arrived back outside the factory about midnight. The day out was the talk of the firm for days and the manager, Mr Pell, organised a letter on behalf of everyone to say thank you to the boss.

Each year after that, I looked forward to the works outings but it was the one in 1953 to the Festival of Britain that was most memorable.

As usual, we boarded the coaches outside the firm, but on this occasion we had an even earlier start. The coaches set off for London at 6am, taking the A6 and A1 roads. We stopped halfway for about half an hour for the usual visits to the toilets but, due to the amount of traffic and getting

through London, we did not arrive at the coach park until after midday. However, we had a long day ahead of us because we were not due to return home until midnight. Our relatives had been advised that we should not be arriving back until about 3.30am.

In the company of a crowd of young women I set off for a few hours in the grand pleasure park. It was a magnificent sight. A giant fun fair, all brightly coloured, noisy and crowded. It was a hot day and we queued for everything. I did not go on the fairground rides because, unfortunately, the swinging up and down and round and around on the covered caterpillar ride made me feel sick, and I did not want to risk spoiling the rest of the day. I ended up holding the coats and handbags of my mates as

Valerie (6th from left on back row) and friends on the Trafford annual outing to the Festival of Britain, 1951. (V. Tedder)

they whirled and twisted on the spinning rides, screaming and thoroughly enjoying themselves. What strong constitutions they had. I enjoyed watching them as much as taking part and we had an hilarious time. We had taken plenty of pocket money with us, but we had not anticipated how expensive the rides and amusements would be. Even the various food snacks were twice the price paid at the seaside. I remember that towards the end of the afternoon, although we had eaten, we had not had a drink. By this time, the group had shrunk, with people wandering off to look at things that interested them. This left four of us and we decided to keep together. We saw a huge sign advertising the sale of cold drinks and made our way through the crowds towards it. We discovered a small tent with tables in front of it laden with bottles of all shapes and sizes, on a white plastic cloth. People were purchasing bottles and taking paper cups. I joined the queue, which seemed to disappear in the crowd for a short distance, while the other three went to find the toilets. We estimated that by the time they returned, I should have been served and ready to hand over the drinks to them. It was a push and shove job all the way to the counter. I persevered and eventually, after a long time, nearly reached the counter. I stood behind several men and tried to see what was on offer. The labels on the bottles were too far away for me to read but the majority around me were pointing to some small green bottles on the right of the table. It seemed a popular choice. Suddenly, there was a voice above the fun fair din, asking who was next. I grasped the opportunity and called out, 'Four of those please,' indicating the small green bottles. I paid an extortionate price, two pounds, and licked my lips in anticipation as the crown tops were prized off and the bottles, with four paper cups, were passed to me. I never thought to read the labels as I pushed my way clear of the crowd and triumphantly made my way to the meeting point. Placing three bottles on the ground, in the shade, I took a long, deep drink from my bottle. The shock made

me shudder and splutter. I then looked at the label. I was drinking DD - Double Diamond beer. It was strong. It tasted bitter and very fizzy. However not being a beer drinker I was not able to tell whether the beer was alright or not. I apologised to my friends when they returned but they were not concerned. A drink was a drink they consoled me, and unflinchingly emptied the bottles. Perhaps they were beer drinkers, I thought, as I slowly sipped mine and quenched my thirst. Before the day was over I drank several bottles of DD and felt quite queasy. I tried to ignore these feelings and a couple of cups of coffee later in the evening made me feel better.

We walked for miles looking at everything and we hardly sat down all day. The attractions and exhibitions were fantastic and it had been a worthwhile visit. Before we knew it the fireworks display was over and it was 11.30pm. We were nowhere near the coach park and feared we would be late back. We checked our money and found that there was sufficient to take a taxi. We hailed a cab in the street and when we told the driver our destination he told us it would take at least twenty five minutes. One friend and I climbed into the back seat. Another pulled down the seat behind the driver and sat down. Our fourth companion climbed in before we had time to pull down the front seat, missed the seat altogether and sat down on the floor. She was stuck with one leg outside the cab and the other bent underneath her. She was not hurt but tipsy enough not to move. When she realised her predicament she burst out laughing and we could not move her. We went into hysterics, pushing and pulling her leg from under her, then doing the same to the other leg and foot stuck out of the taxi door. The driver was no help, just complained and told us to stop messing about. When we had safely dragged her leg inside the cab, we shut the door and the driver drove off immediately, not giving our friend a chance to get up. She remained on the floor all the way to the coach park. I paid the fare while the others extricated the girl from the cab.

The taxi shot off with a loud revving of the engine, leaving us standing there still laughing and crying with hysterics. We dragged our helpless friend along until we located our row of coaches. We were in luck. Ours turned out to be at the end of the queue just about to pull off the coach park. Out of breath and beginning to feel weak from running and dealing with our girlfriend, we clambered aboard the coach to the sound of 'Where have you been?' and 'We were going without you'. We did not care. We stood in the aisle trying to explain what had happened in the taxi but it was so funny we collapsed with laughter again. No one could get any sense out of us and declared we had been drinking. We had but we were not drunk, just full of fun. Absolutely worn out we fell into our seats and within minutes were fast asleep.

I woke up a couple of hours later and saw the glorious moonlight on the fields. It was as bright as day. In addition, there was a ground mist that made everywhere look extremely eerie and ghostly. I watched the scene as we sped along but was soon lulled back to sleep again. The next time I awoke we were on the outskirts of Leicester. This time, I saw the sun coming up and watched as the dawn mist cleared. It was light by the time we parked in Lancaster Street at 4.30am. I wondered what my parents would say, being so late back. When I let myself into the house, Mum was already downstairs. She admitted she had not slept, just dozed until she heard the sound of the coaches as they turned the corner of the street on the way to the factory. She was glad I was safely home. I could not tell her much about my day out because I was so tired. She made me go straight to bed. It was the most wonderful day and, although I went on numerous firm's outings while employed at the Trafford, there was not one that compared with the trip to the Festival of Britain.

Christmas carols

Christmas Eve was always a time for me to get excited and it meant I could stay out a little later at night than usual. The Church organised the Christmas Eve carols and visits to all those people in the parish who had made a request. For weeks we had been practising after the Sunday evening service and we knew all the carols off by heart. In addition to the choir anyone could attend and support the singing. Carols were sung outside the homes of church members and a donation to charity was the reward. I looked forward to the event whatever the weather and always arrived in good time at the schoolroom where we were given a lecture on behaviour, the route we were to walk, given a hymn book and checked to see we each had a torch. At 8pm we would start following the leader as he led us from house to house. We walked everywhere at that time, covering a large area and several miles. It was usually around 1am to 2am when we had finished.

When we arrived in the street in which was the house to be visited, we were told the numbers of the carols to be sung. Then, after a lot of shushing, we quietly approached the house. We formed a circle outside the front door and, after a hum for the correct pitch to commence, we started singing at the drop of a hand. We already knew the carols and, as the old favourites were requested again and again, we would laugh and joke about it. The carols varied by having descants, male solos, female solos and chants. It all sounded very professional. After two carols we would say together, 'Goodnight Mr and Mrs —— and family. Merry Christmas'. Often the door was opened and the family would come out into the street and join in the singing. Frequently we had a street full of onlookers and someone was always quick to pass among them with a collecting box.

During the course of the evening we would make stops at the homes of those who had made arrangements to feed us and give us a drink. It varied from hot soup and hot bread, to hot mince pies and sausage rolls, and lots of sandwiches and cakes. All were most welcome and on cold winter nights we were very glad of the hot food provided.

As far as I was concerned, the group was very tolerant and organised the route so that they could sing carols outside my home then leave me there. They sang Mother's favourite, which was 'O Come All Ye Faithful' and another which had not been sung much during the evening, to help break up the repetition. In the beginning I was usually home by 10pm but, as I grew older, the time was stretched towards midnight, but I was never allowed out after that time. Sadly I would wave my friends goodbye and go in, knowing that the faithful few would continue until the last family on the list had been visited.

We walked many miles on these Christmas Eve events but one year it came to a halt. No more walking. The list was too long and the carolling had to be speeded up. Cars - that was the answer. All those with a car, or who could borrow one for the evening, were recruited to convey the singers around the parish. This became great fun, jumping in and out of any vehicle to hand, especially to those like me whose family did not possess such transport. After several years and when petrol became more expensive, it was decided that all carollers should pay towards the cost of the transport. A coach was booked and the cost equally divided among us. The coach was a 32-seater and ample for our needs. We had lots of fun laughing and joking between the house visits. Sometimes the addresses were so near we did not bother to sit down but just hung onto the seats for the short distance we travelled. A number of the group did their courting on the back seat of the coach but they were always among the group outside the house, supporting the choir. It was all very hilarious at times. Often it was the highlight of my Christmas.

At home, our old piano had seen better days. Purchased cheap from a second-hand shop in Charnwood Street, it was tuned by a blind piano tuner from the

Wycliffe Society for the Blind in Gedding Road, Leicester. The piano was a walnut upright with pretty inlaid wood flower designs set in the centre front behind the drop down music stand. There were numerous stains and chips in the wood, being scars from years of misuse and house moves.

My father, who never had a piano lesson in his life, was an accomplished player learning all the tunes by ear. After many years of tickling the ivories while in the navy he had quite a repertoire. Nothing fancy, but all the well known tunes and choruses were within his range. Everyone enjoyed his simple way of playing.

The piano stood in the living room, and the once smooth, glossy ebony keys were well worn and dull. The ivory keys, cream with age and tinged around the edges with a yellow stain, were showing minute cracks and indentations in the middle of the centre keys, from years of wear. The little hammers attached to the tan leather straps were faded and worn and were being slowly chipped away as they struck the metal wires. Several of the hammers were headless and misshaped. The wires were worn with signs of too much slack and rusty edges around the screws. The brass pedals were both worn thin, dull and crooked with the constant weight of pumping feet. Nevertheless, it was our pride and joy and after a good clean and polish by Dad, it gave us many years of pleasure. He was only too pleased to oblige with a tune when asked.

Christmastime was when the piano gave of its best. Boxing Day was family day and Mum invited several from her large family over for the afternoon and evening. She had five brothers and a sister, all married, some with children, and they would descend on our house for fun and games.

We children usually had the front room to ourselves and were fully occupied playing board games, card and party games, while the adults talked and drank their Christmas cheer in the living room. Sometimes during the afternoon or after the evening meal Dad would fetch out his 'Housey Housey' game for all of us to play together. He made a large board with the numbers painted on it. The counters were white with a red border and a red number. The counters, about the size of a two pence piece, were placed in a soft linen bag and shaken up. We all had a little card with various numbers painted on it and smaller counters to cover up the numbers as they were called. No one was allowed to write on these cards because they had to be used repeatedly. We had great fun with sweets and chocolates for prizes. Often we would break in the middle of a bingo session for a sing-along while glasses were recharged. The meal was usually served about 6pm.

To accommodate such a lot of guests, Mum would move her three foot square dining table to the corner of the room near to the double window, well out of the way. The table was dark oak with gate legs, and both leaves were fully extended. An enormous white linen tablecloth was draped over it and then it was all hands helping to set it with the traditional Christmas fare. In the centre, on a raised glass cake plate, would be Mum's speciality - the Christmas cake. It was home-made, with marzipan and icing usually forked up on the top to look like rough snow, and topped with a Santa Claus, fir tree and a sledge.

When we had all eaten, Dad would top up the glasses, pull up his chair to the piano and start the sing-song. Everyone joined in the selection of old time songs and carols and Dad often played more modern tunes when requested. The old piano did wonders and although the keys gradually began to wear and the notes frequently were out of tune, no one seemed to notice because they were all singing heartily and loudly.

About midnight everyone made a move to return home. Dad and I would help clear up when the last guests had gone. Then came the washing up and putting the house straight before going to bed. Mum could never face the house the next morning after a party, so we worked

Boxing Day party at Nottingham Road (V. Tedder)

until everything was shipshape before retiring.

Years later when the family drifted apart and the parties stopped, Mum and Dad would entertain their friends occasionally. There was one couple, Lily and Syd Wilmott, who came many times. I recall one Boxing Day, Dad started to play the piano about 9pm and Syd, enjoying the chance to sing along, stood beside him for three hours facing the wall singing every song as it came. Mum just kept filling their glasses and they kept going. They were oblivious to all around as they sang to their hearts content.

Gradually, Dad eased off playing and the piano stood untouched. It was too old to be tuned again and became an ornament, a reminder of happy fun days.

One day Mum declared that she was tired of having to clean it and thought that we ought to get rid of it. Dad was reluctant but he agreed it was hardly going to be used again in its state. He knew she was right but he hung onto the memories it held. Eventually Dad became used to the idea and made enquiries to get it removed. He discovered that it cost more than he could afford to have it carted away and set about taking it to pieces himself. His idea was to saw it up into small bits and then burn them in the factory boiler. It turned out to be a tougher job than he anticipated.

George, the other boilerman, assisted with the removal from the house to the back yard. It was pushed, pulled, carried and lifted until it was out of the front door and set down in the gateway. Then Dad set about dismantling it. The piano was well made and resisted the screwdriver. It was not going to go without making objections. At last, after many bangs with the hammer, the casing fell apart. When it came to breaking up the innards, he found an axe and a saw the only tools effective. Over the next few days he managed to break it down into small enough pieces to burn in the boiler. The noise of the piano in its death throws was terrifying. The clungs, clangs, plonks and plangs, together with the screeching of the wires that put our teeth on edge, were tremendous. It objected to the last, and even in the boiler as it burned Dad heard the twang of some of the wires snapping in the heat.

It was a sad ending for such a fine instrument that had given great pleasure. We never purchased another. Dad managed to keep his hand in by playing the piano in a local pub occasionally. He still managed to raise a hearty sing-song from the customers when he played the oldies on the battered, out of tune instrument.

'Hell hath no fury...'

One Saturday morning Mum was furious. She had stepped into the yard to hang out washing on the line when she noticed a large amount of waste paper and litter in the factory drain. It had obviously been blown there overnight. As she glanced around the yard and gateway, she saw the litter was piled against the flower boxes, the dustbin, in another drain and behind the wheels of Dad's bicycle. We were summoned outside to inspect the mess. Mr and Mrs Jackson, our elderly neighbours, heard the commotion and came out to join us. We were at a loss as to how this large amount of waste paper had accumulated. It consisted mainly of dirty brown paper, labels, sweet wrappers, empty and screwed up cigarette boxes and lunch wrappers. Other paper in various colours was torn into small pieces.

Mum declared that on top of everything else we had to put up with from the dye works and the factory hands, we now had their filthy litter to contend with. Dad said that he doubted it was from the dye works because the men usually swept up their rubbish into large bins, and he had the job of emptying them into the boiler and burning it. We all helped to clean up the mess and by the time we had finished we had filled two-thirds of a dustbin.

The following Saturday morning, shortly after opening the gate, we discovered the yard in a similar state. We inspected some of the papers but there was nothing to indicate where it was originating. Again we cleaned up the mess and filled the dustbin.

On the third Saturday, we discovered waste paper and various miscellaneous litter that had blown into a corner of the yard. This time Mum decided to meticulously check it for some clue to indicate who was responsible. Patiently she checked each torn piece or smoothed out the screwed up papers until she finally found a label with an address. The culprits were revealed. Someone at Pollard Engineering Company further along Nottingham Road was depositing the litter in the street. The factory was adjacent to the last house in the block of five. It had a gateway similar to ours, but not usually opened because it gave direct access into the factory. Mum collected every piece of litter, waste wrapping paper and string, and placed it in a large plastic bag. The tell-tale labels she kept separately as proof.

The following Monday morning Mother made herself very presentable, went to the offices of Pollard Engineering and requested an interview with the boss. She took the plastic bag and contents in one hand and the documents of proof in the other. After a number of office staff had seen her and then a short interview with the manager, she at last found herself in the office belonging to the boss of the firm. She told him the story and showed him the waste paper. He was not at all pleased and accused her of making rather a sweeping statement in alleging his firm was to blame. He needed proof. Dramatically, Mum emptied the plastic bag onto his desk. She flourished the labels, wage slips and packets before him. Here was his proof, the name of the firm being on several pieces of the waste papers. He agreed. He was shocked and most apologetic. It was definitely waste from his firm. He promised to deal with the matter and find the culprits immediately. Mother later said that he was very much the gentleman, promising that it would not happen again and escorted her right to the front door of the building, then shaking her hand before she left. Mum had the last word though. She threatened to inform the police the next time it occurred. By the time she had finished her statement she was sure he knew he would be prosecuted. As a reminder, she had left all the dirty smelling waste paper still on his desk.

However we solved the mystery ourselves. It appeared that every Friday evening the men employed at Pollard's swept out the week's waste, including any pay slips or packets that had been thrown down. The workmen responsible for cleaning up opened the gate and swept the mess out into the street. The gate was then closed and the

waste left to blow anywhere around the street. Overnight the wind blew it about and the majority found its way into our gateway.

Mum kept observation for several weeks on a Friday night just in case it happened again, but it did not. The boss kept his word and we had no further trouble. I think Mum must have put the fear of God into him. She had that effect on us many a time.

There was a similar occasion when large bales of wool were stored in our gateway for a few weeks at the request of John Wilson, the dye works boss. Every time the factory workers came to collect some of the parcels of wool from the great sacking bales, they dropped the strings and labels onto the ground. When the sacking bales were empty these too were left just where they dropped. They were dirty and smelt of oil and wool. They were supposed to clean up as they went along but didn't for some reason. Once or twice Mum had to push the sacks to one side so that no one fell over them, especially at night in the pitch black of the gateway. When a few days had elapsed and no effort had been made to remove them, she became very annoyed and decided to deal with the matter her way. She went out and collected all the empty sacks, bits of string and labels and piled them on top of one another on one of the larger sacks. Because the pile was too heavy to carry, she grabbed hold of the two corners and dragged it out of the gateway, along the street and into the factory offices. Ascertaining that Mr Wilson was in his office, she opened wide his door and dragged the sack pile in front of his desk. It meant that if he wanted to leave the office he would have to step over it. He stood flabbergasted while she explained her action. She threatened to have him sued for damages if anyone fell over the sacks in the gateway through the neglect of his workers. She made him promise that they would remove any sacks, labels and ties each time they collected the various bales. She insisted that the gateway was kept clean and tidy for health reasons.

Because our house wall was adjacent to the factory we

Julie in the yard at Nottingham Road, 1948 (V. Tedder)

Moat Road Infants School, she had no trouble settling in. She was a keen pupil and we had already taught her to read and write which made her advanced in her class. How things changed in the household when Julie went to school. No longer did Mum leave the washing, dressing and breakfasting of Julie until I had left for work, now it was all hands to the pump. Most mornings I supervised getting her out of bed, washed and dressed, and left her eating her breakfast as I dashed out of the door to get to work on time. Later Mum would walk Julie to school for 9am. Lunchtime too was never the same. Previously, helping to serve the meal and assisting with the clearing away afterwards made me very much appreciated. The meal had been ready for me when I arrived home from work at 12.40pm and, although I helped clear the table afterwards and performed my daily chore of dusting the living room, Mum usually washed and dried the pots and pans at her leisure after I had returned to work for the afternoon session. Suddenly it became a mad scramble. Mum had to collect Julie from school at midday, return home to complete cooking the meal, eat it and be ready to take her back to school for the afternoon period at 1.30pm. Mum believed in giving us a hot meal and a pudding daily and as the weeks went by, she worked out menus that could be easily prepared and cooked in the shortest possible time. While Dad was employed at Wilson's, Mum usually kept his dinner hot between two plates over a saucepan of boiling water until he was able to leave the boilers and have his lunch break. There was never a set time for him to eat. Later, when he changed his employment and was unable to get home for lunch, he took sandwiches and Mum cooked especially for him in the evening. However, after a family conference when it was decided cooking twice a day was too much for Mum, we started dining together in the evening about 6pm.

Mum was very particular about our clothes and we were kept spick and span. She was very upset one day, when I pointed to a new dress that Julie was wearing, clean

could hear the men shouting remarks about Mum's action. It carried above the noise of the machinery. Dad was told and he had suitable words for the culprits. It seemed to make the employees more conscientious for a time and the property was respected, but within a matter of weeks they started leaving a mess again. It was a continual round of complaints. There was always something new for Mum to complain about and to deal with by challenging the boss to solve the problem. Mum was well aware that the men found her a source of amusement and were very prejudiced against her, but she had to fight for our rights.

It was during this spring that Julie started school. She was only four years old but, when she was accepted at the on ready for school. She had been out into the gateway for some reason and it was drizzling with rain. When she walked into the kitchen, the dress was covered in soot spots and dye smudges. Mum lost her temper and I made matters worse by saying, 'Look, Julie's wearing a Technicolor polka dot dress again'. Mum changed Julie's dress, all the time muttering how difficult it was to keep ahead of the weekly washing despite having a gas boiler and a mangle. Poor Julie, she was pushed and pulled while the dress was removed. Mum shook out the dress and pointed to the various coloured spots. Then removing her apron and telling Julie she would be late for school, she ran out of the house and round to the factory office to see the boss. She knew it was a waste of time and energy lodging her complaint, but she felt she had to keep complaining even though there seemed no way of stopping the problem. Mum certainly had a lot of patience because it took a long time to remove the coloured spots by hand washing, and the garments never looked the same despite her efforts. I kept telling her she ought to contact the Persil Soap Company and to challenge them to create a powder that would easily and gently remove the dye stains.

Julie was never a mischievous child as I had been and never got herself into scrapes. If she did anything wrong I was usually there to stand by her or take her side, despite Mum being very strict and domineering. She was a studious child always with her nose in a book or sorting out puzzles. She was happy reading or writing stories, extremely interested in nature, animals and wildlife. She was a quiet person with not a lot to say. Although there were twelve years and six days between us, we enjoyed one another's company. Unfortunately, there was a generation gap and it was at the time of my life when, as a teenager working long hours and trying to forge out a social life of my own, she was left very much to her own devices. She was just as much an only child as I had been and became an independent person extremely quickly. I spent may hours with her on the allotment, on Spinney Hill Park, and often took her to the cinema, especially the Cameo in High Street. We got on well together. I loved having a sister but being that much older I'm afraid I must have been like a second mother to her. It was to take years for the age gap to close so that we became pals, able to socialise and take holidays together.

Julie on Dad's allotment (V. Tedder)

Tripping the light fantastic

Among the women working on my bench at the Trafford was a young lady in her late twenties. She was black haired, attractive and well proportioned. Although much older than me we struck up a friendship when we discovered a mutual interest in ballroom dancing. I was quite light on my feet and able to do many of the modern sequence dances, having been taught a number of routines as a young girl.

Joan Parker was single and lived at home with her elderly parents, only a short distance from my house. She had been attending a dancing session once a week to improve her abilities and asked me to accompany her. I listened intently to her tales of meeting people, especially young men, dancing partners, learning new dances and thoroughly enjoying herself. It all appealed to me. I did not socialise much outside church activities and saw this as an opening to a better social life. I envied her because my mother would not hear of me going to dance halls. It was not that she was Victorian in her attitude, it was because she was worried about the people I would be associating with and felt she had to keep a strict control on my activities. Any dancing therefore was done in the presence of my parents. At 17^1/$_2$ I thought differently, but until the time came to rebel I abided by their wishes. Goodness knows what she thought I would be getting up to. Anyway, it was not long before the opportunity came for me to start dancing on a regular basis.

My parents had to take a few days' holiday at short notice. I was not able to accompany them due to me being over 17 and past the age of taking time off to accompany parents. I had to take my holiday with everyone else in August. This meant they were obliged to leave me at home to fend for myself. It appeared that the boiler had broken down in the factory next door and needed new parts. Dad

was asked to take leave until the new parts were delivered and installed. They decided to visit my Uncle Archie and Auntie Florrie at Chatham and, of course, took Julie with them. Before leaving, they gave me strict instructions on how to behave, take care of the house and feed myself. However, I had other plans.

I continued working daily and every evening when I returned home, Mrs Jackson, our neighbour, made it her business to call on me. I think Mother put her up to it. One evening I went out to the cinema straight from work with a girl friend and I never thought to mention it to Mrs Jackson. When I returned home just after 10pm, she was waiting in the street, looking for me. I felt embarrassed and apologised. I made a mental note to make sure I informed her in future and hoped she would not tell tales to Mum.

On the Tuesday of that week Joan asked me again if I would like to go dancing with her that night. I had been so brainwashed by my mother that I declined. I felt I could not go behind her back.

The other women backed Joan and eventually persuaded me that I would come to no harm, especially as Joan promised to chaperon me and accompany me home afterwards. It was pointed out that I was old enough to please myself and it was about time I did. So, unable to come up with any excuses not to go, I agreed. Inwardly, I felt quite excited and looked forward to the occasion. Later that day, suitably dressed for the occasion and carrying a pair of silver sandals in a bag, I took the bus to Victoria Park gates on London Road, where I had arranged to meet Joan at 7.30pm. From there we crossed the road and entered the Casino dance hall.

The dances were organised by two retired professional dancers, Ted and Vera Holt. Admission was two shillings and sixpence and included a 45 minute lesson and a 15 minute interval. The last waltz was at 10pm. This gave us just enough time to catch the penultimate bus home from the corner of Evington Road and London Road,

As I followed Joan up the very narrow staircase to the

ballroom on the first floor, I could hear the lively dance music which I discovered came from a small gramophone at the end of the room. I was pleasantly surprised when I walked into the ballroom. It was lightly decorated and the wooden dance floor shone from end to end. White chalk had been scattered onto the floor which assisted the sliding of the feet during the dancing. All around the walls was a single row of chairs mostly occupied by a mixed bunch of people, and there were plenty of male partners. Some were in their twenties and looked most pleasant. I changed my shoes and hung up my coat in the small cloakroom on the second floor. As soon as I returned to the ballroom I was asked to dance by a nice young man and, as the evening progressed, I realised what I had been missing. A number of couples were regulars and assisted Ted and Vera during the tuition period. They encouraged us and before the evening came to a close, I told Joan I would be attending regularly with her. The crowd were a decent bunch, very jolly and only interested in learning to dance properly. Joan kept her promise to see me home.

When my parents returned I waited for the right opportunity to tell them about the dancing. Mum was angry that I had gone behind her back and I was sorry for the deceit. She accused Joan of leading me astray, being a man hunter, and said she was far too old to be my friend. We had a row about it until Dad intervened. He said that if it was something I wanted to do he saw no harm in it, as long as I behaved myself with the men I met and was home by 10.30pm. Mum reluctantly agreed. From then on I attended each week.

As we learned new steps and improved our dancing techniques, Joan and I would go into fits of laughter when we fell over our partners' feet. Sometimes, if we partnered a slow witted male with two left feet, we would stifle grins and hold back the giggles and pull faces at one another behind their backs as we struggled around the dance floor. On the other hand I met some lovely lads and had some marvellous partners. Often there were some men who

would only dance a specific dance with a female partner. I had mine, three to be exact. One for each of the waltz, quickstep and foxtrot.

I recall there was one little man, a head shorter than me, about fifty years of age who always asked me for a waltz. He took several minutes making the request because he stammered, but I waited patiently for him to finish before consenting.

Then there was the tall, fair haired young man, obviously conscious of his good looks and smelling of *Old Spice* aftershave, who always asked me to dance a quickstep with him to show off his ability, not mine. He would literally spin me around and around the floor from one end to the other until I was quite dizzy. After I learned the feather step I would grin behind his back at Joan as we sped across the dance floor. I frequently collapsed out of breath after a dance with him.

We all joined in the old favourite, the 'Paul Jones'. It mixed up the dancers, making us dance with whoever stood in front of us when the music stopped. We had some very amusing partners and learned which ones were to be avoided.

It was during one of these Tuesday sessions that I fell in love for the first time. Two young soldiers stationed at Saffron Lane Barracks arrived one night in uniform, eager to learn to dance. When they arrived they were wearing their heavy, black boots and were advised to bring proper lightweight dancing shoes on their next visit. And they did. We watched as they changed their boots for black patent leather shoes. Both of them could dance but wanted to improve their standard.

One of the soldiers, aged 21, tall with black wavy hair and very polite, took a shine to me and became my partner during the lessons. We did a great foxtrot together. After several weeks in his company he asked if he could take me home one night. I thought I knew him well enough to trust him and agreed. I told Joan who understood the situation and wished me luck. With his arm around my waist he waited at the bus stop with me, then travelled home with me, paying my bus fare and then walking me to the front gate. He gave me a peck on the cheek and arranged to see me the following week. I realised just how keen he was because after leaving me he had a six mile walk back to the barracks. I knew that on his small wage he would not take a taxi. We kept up the association for several weeks going dancing and to the cinema occasionally. Each time he took me home afterwards. I succumbed to a couple of passionate kisses and he was eager for me to be his regular girlfriend. I was elated. This was the first time anyone had really taken a liking to me and to have a boyfriend to talk about was wonderful. Then one week he failed to turn up. I was unable to contact him and after three weeks had passed decided he must have changed his mind about me. I was devastated and very upset. I always like a reason for finishing friendships. Joan was aware of the situation but I told my workmates we had had an argument. Then Joan had a friend who knew a friend, and eventually it was discovered that he and his pal had gone with their Unit to Germany at short notice. I never saw him again. I felt heartbroken and let down. My parents, unaware of my friendship with Ian, wondered what had come over me when I declared I was not going dancing at the Casino ever again. I did not tell them the reason. Joan consoled me across the workbench and encouraged me to keep going to the dances. It was all part of life's disappointments and I would no doubt meet someone else more considerate. I took her advice and continued, but I was very wary from then on and did not get involved with anyone else for a long time.

A few months later, having gained experience on the dance floor, Joan and I decided to branch out. We had noticed in the local evening paper, advertisements concerning special dances held at the Palais de Danse on Friday evenings and often there was a ball at the De Montfort Hall on a Friday night. The public were allowed to attend these dances subject to the availability of tickets.

Joan proposed that we continued the Tuesday night sessions and, when we could afford it, go to one of the big dances in town. At that time, during the autumn and winter months and especially around Christmas and the New Year, numerous large firms in the city held dances for the works' employees. The dances were so popular that it was nigh impossible to gain admission by paying at the door on the night.

We chose our first dance. It was the Everard's Ball at the Palais. The price of the tickets was seven shillings and sixpence. However, the first hurdle was telling Mother. By now Dad was no problem. When I outlined our proposal it was met with utter disapproval. Dancing in town on Friday night and late home. No! Every conceivable reason was put forward to discourage me from going. Wasn't I satisfied with one night a week?

Eventually, after raising the subject a couple of times and as the date of the dance drew near, Mum relented but not until I had been subjected to a long lecture on how to behave with any lad or man wanting more than just a couple of dances. She put her foot down. No lads were to be brought home. I was far too young to be involved. Having agreed I could go, she laid down a final condition. I was to come home in a taxi afterwards. There was no walking home alone. I agreed. Later Joan and I had an agreement. Neither of us could afford a taxi on top of the dance tickets so we would walk home together. Should either of us meet and strike up a friendship with a fellow and they wanted to escort us home, the one left would take a taxi home alone. For the time being I was satisfied, having permission to go out dancing wherever I chose until midnight. Before I left the house, Mother would check that I had a pound note in my possession to cover the cost of the cab. In case I had my small evening purse stolen at the dance, I wrapped the pound note in a small lace handkerchief and placed it inside my elasticated knicker leg, for emergencies.

We attended many of the special dances, the Candy

Ball, Press Ball, Corah's Ball, Gent's Ball and the Police Ball. Joan would obtain the tickets in advance so I was always committed to go with her. The dances entailed more glamorous outfits. Long evening dresses were out and the short cocktail dresses in. I saved my pocket money and purchased suitable evening material and made my own dresses. Often after lunch I would sneak back to work early, and for about twenty minutes use the works machine to complete a garment. I saved up two pounds and bought one of the first pair of wedge-heeled gold dance shoes on sale in the city. I was the envy of all my girl friends.

I recall two special dresses that I painstakingly made.

Both were of the new A-line design with three-quarter length sleeves and a dropped waistline. One was in mauve and pink taffeta and the other a pale turquoise shot silk. Joan and I were always ahead in the fashions, wearing our outfits in rotation. Afterwards came the long straight skirts worn with frilly blouses.

One Saturday I was looking around C & A Modes Limited in Granby Street, when I spotted a plain slim fitting black skirt. It was calf length and had a black velvet heart shaped pocket on the right hip. The pocket was scattered with tiny rhinestones in a criss-cross pattern. I mentioned it to Mum when I went home and told her this was the new

Granby Street, Leicester (Leicester City Council)

fashion. Imagine my surprise when I arrived home from work one day in the week to find that Mum had been into town and bought it for me. I could hardly believe it. She was showing interest in my dancing clothes. This purchase was followed shortly afterwards with two frilly blouses that she had seen in the town and thought would go well with the skirt. One was pink with lace around the collar and cuffs and black buttons down the front. The second was a white nylon blouse with tiny pearl buttons down the front and a black satin bow at the neck. The sleeves were very full and pulled tightly into a small wristband. Both went well with the skirt and I wore them on alternate weeks. I never sat down in my skirt and only wore it on dance nights. I felt very glamorous in my fashionable clothes.

It was a pleasure going to the Palais. The ballroom was large and always crowded. There were two stages, one upper and one lower. The lower usually housed the resident band or a visiting band, and the upper stage had a small group of two or three musicians to play during the breaks. Both decks were surrounded by flowers and plants and subdued lighting. In the centre of the ballroom was a fountain about five feet high. This too was surrounded by flowers and plants and had fine sprays of water playing in the centre from small jets around the sides. It was lit by coloured lights and looked very attractive. People would dance around the fountain in a clockwise direction. In the ceiling was a large mirror ball and, when the spot light was played onto it, the reflection around the dance hall and on the fountain was fantastic. All around the room was a balcony with chairs and tables set so that folk could watch the dancers while they took refreshment. Coffee, tea and soft drinks were available, but the bar was situated in a more secluded area at the far end. I recall there was a large statue of a knight in shining armour near the access door to the bar. Although Joan drank rum and orange, I never did. I kept to soft drinks or tea. It was during one of these special dances that I met my second heart throb and went all of a twitter again.

I had danced a number of quicksteps with him and we went well together. He told me his name was Brian. He was tall, slim, smart, good looking and charming. He asked to take me home after the dance but I refused. I wanted to get to know him better. We arranged a date and I met him a couple of times on cinema expeditions. He was quite the gentleman and began taking me home afterwards. He gave me a peck on the cheek before arranging a date to see me again. I was thrilled. I had really fallen for this one.

A few weeks later I told him that Joan and I were going to the De Montfort Hall to the Victor Silvester Ball. He turned up there giving me a nice surprise. We danced all evening together and when it was time to go home, Joan who had a new acquaintance, was offered a lift home in his car, so I agreed to let Brian walk me home. We left the De Montfort Hall about midnight and walked quickly to my house. When we reached my gateway we stood outside for a few minutes fixing up another date. Brian then took me in his arms and kissed me. Suddenly the wicket-gate opened and my mother was standing there. She stepped through the gate pointing her finger at Brian and told him to get off home. What time did he call this? She smacked my face and ordered me into the house. We were so surprised we obeyed. As Brian went quickly down the street he called out, 'Bye. See you Wednesday', and was gone in the darkness. I screamed and cried in despair as I was pushed down the gateway and into the back door. How could she show me up like that? What had I done wrong? I knew by the look of horror on Brian's face I should be lucky if I saw him again. My mother's explanation was feeble. She had heard us walking up the street and had waited for me to go in. When I did not go in immediately, she came out to see what we were doing. When she saw us kissing she put a stop to it immediately. She said it was because I was outside too long instead of getting in home. I was absolutely shocked. We had done nothing to be ashamed of or to warrant her outburst. We had only stood outside for about five minutes, if that. I could not believe it had happened. I was eighteen years of age and had my face smacked, a stinging wallop, because I had a boyfriend. We argued for days and I rebelled against my mother's interference. Even Dad said that she had gone too far and that I was old enough to look after myself. Mum was always one to hit first and ask questions later.

I never understood why my mother had acted the way she did. She was the last person to query my behaviour. She met Dad at a friend's wedding when she was 15 years of age, became engaged to him at 17 and married at 19. I could not forgive her. It was so embarrassing and humiliating. When I went to work on the following Monday morning I told Joan what had happened. She in turn told the women on the bench and everyone sympathised with me. They were disgusted and I was advised to leave home.

At home I went about in silence. I could not hold a conversation with my mother. I was ashamed of her behaviour in front of Brian and wondered what he was going to say when I met him. I need not have bothered. He did not turn up at the cinema on the Wednesday evening. I could not bring myself to accept that Mother had driven him away, but after waiting for nearly two hours outside the Odeon cinema in Queen Street, I knew he was not going to see me again. When I arrived back home and told Mother he had not turned up, she said, 'Well, if he had been all that keen on you he would have'. I went to bed crying. All I could see were those beautiful brown eyes of his, staring in amazement, first at me then at Mother before he turned away and left. I never forgave her.

I saw Brian several times at a couple of dance halls and tried to apologise for my mother's behaviour, but I knew there was nothing I could do to repair the damage she had caused between us. Apart from the odd waltz and an enquiry about my state of health, he kept clear of me and after a word or two with his mates, they also kept away from me. I made a vow, and stuck to it for years, that I would never take a young man home or anywhere near my mother until I was sure of what I was doing. Casual

boyfriends were kept a secret.

It took me some time to recover from this sad state of the heart, but I was determined to continue the dancing sessions. From then on, Joan and I visited many dance halls around the city including the one above the fire station in Lancaster Road, the one above the Co-operative store on Uppingham Road, the Regency on London Road and the Trocadero on Scraptoft Lane.

Years later Joan met a young man at one of the dances and became engaged to him. After a short engagement they were married at the Catholic Church on Mere Road and I was her bridesmaid. I had plenty of young men friends and dancing partners but I steered clear of getting involved with any of them. I kept a tight rein on my feelings.

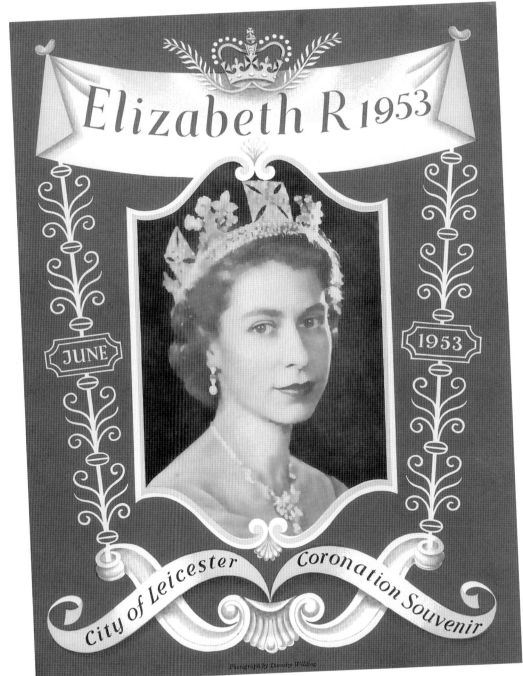

Elizabeth R 1953

JUNE

1953

City of Leicester Coronation Souvenir

Photograph by Dorothy Wilding

CHAPTER SIX

The Coronation

On the morning of 6 February 1952, we heard over the radio the sad news of the death of King George VI. He had died of cancer at Sandringham. Within hours flags were flown at half mast and in some cases black flags erected. Pictures of the late King were displayed in banks, shops and businesses were draped with a black cloth or ribbons, and everyone went about their daily chores and duties in quiet respect.

The King and Queen Elizabeth were greatly admired because of their decision to remain in London during the war. They had made themselves akin to their subjects by visiting the bombed out areas in and around London, and especially when Buckingham Palace received a direct hit by a bomb and they refused to leave their home. The nation seemed to take the loss of the King to heart and we all felt a sadness and sympathy for the Royal Family.

The young Princess Elizabeth, at the age of 25, was proclaimed Queen Elizabeth the Second. She was in Kenya with her husband Prince Philip when the news of her father's death reached her, and she returned home immediately.

The state funeral of the late King was broadcast over the radio and we listened to the description of the scene by the commentators, who made such a good job of it we could see in our mind's eye the gun-carriage carrying the coffin draped with the Royal Standard flag and his Royal Appointments laid on the top. The coffin was followed by Kings, Heads of State, Prime Ministers, and representatives from countries overseas. These were followed by a long procession of members of the Armed Services. The crowds lining the route to Westminster Abbey stood in silence, and the atmosphere of the occasion came across on the radio as if we were actually taking part in the event. It was very sad but a marvellous tribute to a well respected man and king.

At the end of the week a film of the funeral was shown at the Cameo cinema before large audiences. There were many in tears as they left the cinema.

We learned of the forthcoming coronation of the Queen which was fixed for 2 June 1953. The arrangements were put into action and for 12 months we watched the City of London prepare for the great day. Weekly announcements were made on the radio and in the newspapers covering the various stages, as platforms were erected, large model lions and unicorns, crowns and shields were hung on lamp posts and on specially built hoardings along the route from the Palace to Westminster Abbey. As the great day drew near the atmosphere built up to such a pitch of excitement that we were hardly able to contain ourselves. We had been given a day's holiday to celebrate and once again the television coverage was the main topic.

By this time a great number of people had television sets, but we were not one of them. Only one of Mum's relatives had purchased a television set and that was her brother George. He and his wife Pat lived in a house on Fosse Road, opposite the recreation ground. We received an invitation to go for the day and watch the coronation on their set. How exciting. Julie was old enough to appreciate the magnitude of the event and through school was well up on the traditions and ceremony to take place. She had been given a cardboard cut-out of the Imperial Stage Coach on a stand, which she had successfully put together. It took pride of place on the sideboard at home for months.

We left home at 9am on 2 June and travelled to Auntie Pat's home. We had been asked to go early because the coverage on the television had started at 6am, showing the crowds along the route and all the trimmings and bunting that covered buildings in and around London. Auntie Pat did not wish us to miss anything. She arranged

Julie and Valerie in 1953 (V. Tedder)

all the meals for that day.

When we arrived her front lounge was packed. Chairs had been placed side by side around the room, cushions were on the floor, and the television, 14 inches in size, was in the centre in front of closed curtains. A small table lamp stood on a dresser at the back of the room. The picture was black and white and we sat stunned in amazement as the picture swept over the crowds and followed the procession, then the royal coach, and finally the Queen as she stepped out to enter the Abbey. We followed the proceedings in silence, broken only occasionally with an 'Oh' or an 'Ah'. We dare not leave the room in case we missed something. Auntie Pat supplied us with drinks and sandwiches periodically, but to this day I cannot remember what we ate or drank. We were absolutely enthralled with the occasion and when it was time to go home in the evening our eyes smarted from the constant staring at the screen. The pictures were not perfect and frequently stars and white dashes flashed across the screen. It had not mattered that such interference had taken place, we had witnessed for the first time in history the coronation of a sovereign in all its splendour and pageantry and we had missed nothing. The news that the event had been filmed in full colour, to be shown on the cinemas, was met with great excitement. We could hardly wait to sit through it all again.

A few weeks later the film of the coronation was shown in its entirety at the Odeon cinema. I took Julie, and the real splendour of the occasion came when we saw it in colour. The jewels and gold sparkled and the richness of the colours was indescribable. The film was fantastic and we all appreciated what a marvellous and extravagant affair it had been. We realised that the event had done much to put Britain on the tourist map. The street decorations alone were wonderful and ingenious. They were left in place for months after the event in order to attract visitors. It had made us long to possess a television set as soon as possible, but finances were such that we were not able to purchase one. It was to be another four years before we rented a set from Radio Rentals in the High Street.

'Time is money'

During the spring of 1953 the thing that I had dreaded the most occurred. My previous experience of being on short time and having to sign on the dole was a stark memory and one I did not want repeated. When the news spread through the works that the factory hours were to be cut for a couple of months due to the lack of orders and a slump in the trade, I took the news badly.

I enjoyed working at the Trafford and the prospect of moving towards my goal as a sample hand was slow, but not out of reach. The thoughts of seeking another job and starting all over again were very daunting. I was quite upset at having half wages and moped and worried for days. Nothing concrete came of the rumour for a couple of weeks and we began to think the firm had risen above such a step. Mum was no help in consoling me. She reasoned that if my wages were greatly reduced through short time there was no alternative but to find another job. She and Dad could ill afford to subsidise my wages.

Then one Friday the forelady told us to stay behind in the canteen after our afternoon tea break. She gave us the news we dreaded. Our hours of work were cut to 9am to 4pm, a loss of three hours a day, every day until further notice. It was bad enough but I was naive to believe that by working harder and faster during the hours we were there I could keep up a decent rate of pay to tide me over the period. I decided to give it a try for a couple of weeks. The more experienced women said that it usually only lasted about a month. Accepting a cut in wages and gritting my teeth, I knuckled down to machining as fast as I could and wasted no time whatsoever. A week later, it suddenly occurred to me that the part-timers, and there were two such married ladies working on our bench, were not losing any time at all. Their hours were 9am to 4pm and they were still going home at the end of the week with a full wage packet. Whispering and discussions in the ladies toilet

and in the canteen behind their backs was noticeable, but no one appeared to want to take up the matter with the management. Everyone agreed it was not right but no one felt the urgency to complain. Tactfully, one woman put the suggestion to the part-timers that they ought to offer to cut their hours but this was met with shrugs and 'It's nothing to do with us or you. If they want to cut us down they will say so'. And that was that. I felt strongly about the unfairness of the situation. Most of the women on the bench said little. They had husbands who could afford to keep them when there was no work. We single girls were the losers and needed full time employment to keep ourselves above the breadline.

Feeling as I did, I sat and brooded. I worried for days at the injustice. Then I felt compelled to make a stand and do something. Plucking up courage, I went along to see the forelady and told her of my concern and complained. She listened but said very little and agreed to take my complaint to the management. I was surprised she had taken it so well. I was unable to report back to my colleagues any favourable result other than it was being looked into. I was told that I had wasted my time and the part-timers grinned and worked harder than ever.

The following day after lunch break the part-timers were called into the canteen. There was a lot of speculation but I was sure it meant that their turn had come for short time. About fifteen minutes later they returned to the workroom. Their faces showed annoyance as they related how they were to go on short time. Taking a cut in hours to match ours, they were to work from 9am to 12 midday until further notice. One or two sent me to Coventry and were very nasty when I spoke to them about work matters. The full-timers on the other hand thanked me. I had done us all a favour.

The union representative was not at all pleased when she discovered what had taken place. She delayed me after work and pointed out that any grievance should have been given to her to resolve. I'm afraid I told her where to get off. She knew the situation and had failed in her duty. In those days, at the age of 18, it was quite something to stand up against the management for factory rights. I risked being sacked on the spot. They could easily have found some excuse. They could pick and choose employees, especially when there was shortage of work. I was considered by some a very brazen hussy and others were shocked that a mere junior should make such a stand for rights. Some were very outspoken saying I was a troublemaker. The majority were grateful and appreciated my interference.

The short time lasted for about eight weeks and I managed to maintain a decent wage that far exceeded my dole money. Tightening my belt and being very economical, the rough period did not last long and soon became just an inconvenient episode when orders suddenly increased and we were back to normal with a vengeance. Before we had got used to the normal regular hours again we were asked to do overtime. I jumped at the chance, working an additional one and a half hours each day, and working Saturday mornings from 8am to 12 midday. It was an extra day's pay every week for about a month and soon made up for the loss of wages incurred only a few weeks before.

It was about this time that I had my first industrial accident. Working on a large conveyor belt industrial machine, accidents were to be expected as there was little one could do to protect the fingers against the sharp needle. It was a well known fact that all newcomers to the trade were warned, but experience convinced one that until a finger had been caught in the machine you did not become a skilled machinist. It was an accident to be avoided but we were all caught eventually. I kept my fingers well away from the needle as it raced up and down. I did not wish to experience a needle through my finger just to prove a point. One day, I was distracted from my work and for a split second averted my eyes from the centre point of the needle as the work travelled between the foot and the teeth. Instantly an excruciating pain shot through the

end of a nail and finger of my right hand as the needle mercilessly penetrated. The shooting pain was accompanied by a loud 'Ouch', which aroused the attention of my workmates. The shock to the system was indescribable. It made me feel instantly sick. I had pulled my finger away from the needle which held fast about a third of the way in. One of the women on the bench stopped the machinery and with a small screwdriver, extricated the needle from the machine before pulling it out of my finger with a pair of pliers. There was very little blood, but soreness and the ensuing black blood blister under the nail was a strong reminder to watch out in future. Soon I was helping others to remove needles from fingers, often broken off when the hand jerked itself away. I became quite hardened to this operation and performed it many times without raising a hair.

There was one young girl who was unable to remove her finger from the machine because the needle had gone right through, trapping the finger between the foot and the teeth. The only way was to pull up the needle through the finger until it cleared the teeth before unscrewing it from the socket. To ensure that the needle didn't travel down any further, one used the adjacent machine to work the needle up and down to match the position of the offending machine, so that when the wheel was turned the needle travelled upwards and not down, which would have caused more pain and distress. I found the exact place the needles matched and carefully noting the way to turn the wheel, stood behind the girl ready to extricate the needle. Another employee held her finger and wrist rigid while I slowly turned the wheel. I was very relieved when the needle moved upwards. As soon as it cleared the teeth I unscrewed the needle and removed her finger from the machine. The girl fainted with the shock and pain and while she was supported by colleagues in this state, I picked up the pliers and pulled out the needle.

We soon recovered from these finger wounds but it was very difficult working with a plaster around the end of the finger. The bruised nails lasted for weeks until the unsightly blood blister beneath them grew out. In some cases, the fingers and nails became misshaped. One thing about these accidents, they were reportable but we always continued to work. Time was money

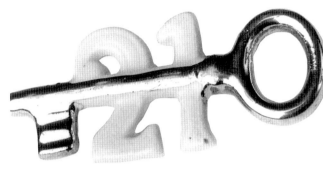

'The key of the door'

A 21st birthday was something to look forward to. It was the official coming of age, the time for receiving the key of the door, and a day to celebrate. My 21st was on a Saturday and my parents had arranged a wonderful day for me. As it turned out it became the worst day of my life. An horrendous day. I have always been glad that we only have one 21st in a lifetime. I would not wish a day like I had on my worst enemy. Things were so bad that I was eventually reduced to tears.

Plans had been made well in advance. My parents had offered me a party or a present, funds would not run to both. Well, I wanted a party. So many of my friends were celebrating their 21st birthdays by having parties, so I chose a party.

My first disappointment came when I was refused the use of the schoolroom at the Church of Christ, Evington Road. The majority of my friends attended there and it seemed the right place for a celebration as it had been my church for a number of years. I met a couple of the church wardens and outlined the programme of events. As soon as I mentioned sherry for the toast and wine with the meal, they shook their heads in disapproval. Sorry, no alcohol. I was mystified. Surely wine or sherry for the toast was customary. It was explained that the actual schoolroom wall was the church wall and all alcoholic drinks were banned. I recalled that several of my friends had held their parties at home or at another community hall. Only one had held his at the church schoolroom and I remembered there was no alcohol supplied for the toast. We drank his health in orange juice. No matter I thought, I would find somewhere. My parents agreed. There was to be a mixture of relatives, family friends and my personal friends at the party, and they felt they had to cater for other people's needs if only by supplying a glass of wine with the meal and sherry for the toast.

It was not as easy as I thought locating a small hall to accommodate my select number of guests. A friend of my father's suggested the schoolroom belonging to St Saviour's Road Church, often leased for social events at a reasonable price. The verger was located and agreed to let us rent the room on the Saturday of my birthday, 2 July. He stipulated that wine could be served with the meal and a glass of sherry for the toast, but no other alcohol was to be consumed on the premises. It was only because the building was not actually attached to the church that this concession was given. Happy to accept the terms, I booked the room from 5pm to 10.30pm.

Next came booking the outside caterers. Mum found a suitable firm who provided everything, pots, cloths, napkins, glasses, cake tray and knife, and the food. To keep the price down I opted for a cold meal. At the time most people had sit down meals even when there were only salads and sandwiches. I chose a menu to compliment a warm summer evening that would please most of the guests. It

was a mixed fruit starter, cold beef and chicken with hot new potatoes, and several mixed salads and pickles. There were small bread rolls and butter, and trifle or gateaux with fresh cream for dessert. This was to be followed by birthday cake and coffee. A light white wine, just one glass per person, and enough sherry for one glass each, was to be purchased by Dad. It all seemed acceptable and the firm verified that the caterers would arrive at the schoolroom at 5pm to set out the tables and food. The guests were arriving at 6.30pm and everything had to be ready by then, although we were not sitting down to dine until 7pm.

Next came the ordering of the cake. I had been advised by a woman at work that two maiden ladies, who lived on East Park Road, were excellent cooks who made and decorated wedding and birthday cakes as a hobby. Many brides had taken advantage of their skill and it would not be too expensive. I took her word for it and one night went to the house to see if they could make and ice a cake to my requirements. They were a charming couple who sat me down and showed me an album of photographs of the cakes they had made. I was very impressed and told them what I wanted. I chose a square cake covered in white icing. All around the edges and corners was a fine lattice-work of scrolls and triangle shapes. On the top I wanted a little shelf so I could stand or lean a gold key with the number twenty one across the centre. They agreed and I paid my deposit of one pound.

I was rather taken aback when one of the ladies went to a drawer and returned with a slip of paper. On it was written all the ingredients required for the rich fruit cake and the icing. I was to purchase everything on the list and take it to them on the date fixed for making the cake. So I did all the shopping and on the date given I went to their house armed with a basket containing everything they had ordered. All I paid them for was their skill in making and

The 'key' card signed by the guests at the party.
(V. Tedder)

decorating the cake.

During the week before my birthday I acquired a large tin from the bakery around the corner and went to collect my cake. It was magnificent. I was well pleased with their handiwork. It looked so beautiful and professional. I nearly had heart failure carrying it home in the tin, frightened to death I might trip up and break it. It seemed a long way home that night as I walked very slowly with my precious parcel. The following day we fetched Mum's old-fashioned Brownie box camera and took several photographs of the cake which we set up on a stool in the yard. When the photographs were developed they did not do the cake justice. The sun was too bright and the intricate lattice-work was lost in a white blur.

The next arrangement was the invitation to my godmother, Ruby, who lived in Rainham. She accepted our request to come and stay from Friday evening until Monday morning. I liked her immensely and looked forward to her visit. In addition Mum had been notified, unbeknown to me, that several friends would be calling at the house on the Saturday morning to bring flowers, cards and presents. With all this in mind, Mum went to Wilson's office to pay the rent the week before my birthday. The boss made some comments about the influx of work and commented on the fact that to cover the extra overtime he had ordered an extra delivery of coal. The yard near our house was to be cleared of the old dye drums and the rubbish burned so that the extra delivery could be dropped in that part of the factory premises. The boilerman would have to remove it a wheelbarrow at a time when it was needed. He apologised in advance for any mess that would be incurred. Mum grasped this opportunity to inform him that it was my 21st birthday the following Saturday, that there would be guests calling during the morning for various reasons and that there would be relatives staying for the weekend. Mr Wilson stated that the coal would not be delivered until the following Monday or Tuesday, so there was nothing for her to worry about. Mum was suspicious

and did not trust his word. He had let us down so many times before over matters concerning the factory. We did not really object to the load of coal being delivered, but past experience showed just how much dust and dirt it caused and Mum did not want that on my day.

Mum went round to see the boss on the Friday afternoon to remind him of my special day and to check on the day the coal was to be delivered. 'All in hand,' he said with a smile, 'No worries. Delivery will be Monday morning'. We all felt relieved.

On Saturday morning I was quite excited. The postman had delivered a large post and I had cards from friends, relatives and workmates. Breakfast was delayed while I opened the post and it must have been about 9am when we sat down at the table to eat. Suddenly there was the loud noise of a motor engine revving up and down and the room went quite dark. We looked out of the bay window and saw a lorry reversing. The blue exhaust smoke clouded by the window and we thought the lorry was coming into the room because it was so close. We sat open mouthed, watching the lorry slowly pass by the window and stop with a jolt. The rear end was near to the factory gates. The lorry was so big it completely obstructed the windows and was so wide there was only a matter of three or four inches between the lorry and the window boxes on each side of the yard. Mum screamed out and rushed from the room yelling that Mr Wilson was a devil. She was unable to get out of the back door to speak to the driver and had to stay on the kitchen step shouting and calling to him. He did not hear because the next thing we heard and saw was the rear end of the lorry tipping up and the coal sliding out onto the ground near to the factory gates. Someone had quietly opened the gates ready for the delivery but had not told us about it. The rush of the coal onto the ground caused a great cloud of dust and within seconds the coal was dumped half in and half out of the gates. No one thought to move our dustbin and it was half buried under the coal. On completion of the delivery the lorry began to move forward up the gateway towards the street. As it moved, the rear end which tipped up began its slow journey back down again. This rear portion only just missed hitting the top of the gateway, the part of the house which was our back bedroom over the gateway. Mother was so angry, but she had to wait until the lorry was back in the street before she could speak to the driver. He denied all knowledge of the delivery scheduled for Monday morning. It was not his fault as he was obeying instructions and had dropped the coal where he had been instructed. Mum then rushed into the factory and checked the offices. No one was there, not Mr Wilson, his partner or his foreman. Only George who had been instructed to open the gates prior to the delivery. He was not aware of any arrangements for Monday. And he had been told that we knew all about it. Mum was so upset she walked up and down the living room threatening all sorts of things against Mr Wilson next time she saw him.

Dad, in the meantime, fetched a shovel and spent the next couple of hours in company with George shovelling coal inside the factory yard out of the way so that we could close the gates on it. He was just as cross as Mum and stated his intention to take up the matter with the boss on Monday.

I was quite upset but it was too late. All we could do was to help Mum clean and dust the house. The kitchen was covered in coal dust and took some time cleaning. The toilet outside I cleaned, and washed down the floor. It was nearly lunchtime before we had finished. Every now and again I had to stop what I was doing to entertain a caller bringing me a gift or card. Instead of being washed, dressed and respectable, I was dirty, hot and dishevelled. I felt embarrassed and knew the day was already going wrong. And that was that. We had never had coal delivered down our gateway prior to that day or afterwards. Mother was convinced it had been done deliberately, and in view of the fact that it was the one and only time, I think she was right.

Mr Wilson acted shocked when he was confronted with Mum's complaint on the Monday morning, and he claimed that he had definitely instructed the coal merchant that delivery was not to be made until Monday. He apologised but we all knew otherwise.

At 5pm, washed but not dressed in my party outfit, I went round to the schoolroom to meet the caterers and to make sure everything we ordered was provided and to indicate the top table and the place settings. I was to be away for a matter of about half an hour. The verger had arranged for the long trestle-tables to be erected and the chairs provided. The kitchen was already opened up and the large tea urns filled ready for the caterers' use. All I had to do was put a few flowers in tiny vases, ready to be placed on the tables when the cloths had been laid.

At 5.45pm I was still there and alone. The caterers had not arrived. I was beginning to panic because there was no one to help me or to ring up the firm to ask where they were. At 6pm Dad arrived. I was nearly in tears. He was dressed in his best suit ready for the party and had come round to see why I was taking so long. He knew I had to complete my dressing and be back to greet the guests at 6.30pm. He assured me all would be well and sent me home.

What a rush! I dashed in, dressed, applied a little make-up, did my hair and rushed back to the schoolroom in time to meet the first arrivals. The caterers were there, laying the tables and setting out the food while my guests were being greeted. What a hustle and bustle. It was a wonder there was not an accident as waitresses bobbed in and out of the guests with plates of food and glasses of wine. The woman in charge of the caterers said that they had been told to arrive at 6pm. It was beyond her control that it was the wrong time. By 7pm and a miracle, everything was ready. No, there came another hitch.

I had engaged a man and his wife from the church who were experts at arranging party games and dances. He arrived with his wife and a friend. The friend was from out of town to attend something to do with the church on the Sunday, and was staying with them as their guest. They knew he was coming but did not think to inform us. We had to wait while another place setting was arranged and everyone moved up a place so that he could sit down next to his hosts. By now, my nerves were beginning to feel quite stretched and I felt that a party had been a bad decision.

At last we sat down to eat and the meal was excellent. Then came the cutting of the cake, serving of the sherry and the speeches. Dad made a lovely speech about his elder daughter and one of the guests stood up to thank my parents for the invitation, the meal and the forthcoming entertainment. Amidst applause I stood to thank everyone for coming and for the lovely presents. It had all been too much, I burst into tears. Mother leaned forward and suggested the kitchen would be a good place to spend a few moments composing myself. I made an excuse and left the table. As I entered the kitchen I saw one of the waitresses placing a bottle of sherry into a holdall. Others were drinking sherries and finishing off the wine bottles. In the corner of the kitchen another waitress, having cut the cake and served small portions on a plate to our guests, was in the process of cutting a quarter of what was left, wrapping it in a serviette and placing it in her bag. I was disgusted and with tears streaming down my face rushed back into the main hall and told my mother. She went into the kitchen and sorted them out, threatening to report them to the firm. We had intended to offer them sherry and to give them a piece of cake but they took it as if it was their right and we were very angry. As for me, it was the last straw. The

day had been ruined one way or another and I wept on and off for the rest of the evening. I found out later that some of the men went out for a pint at The Rifle Butts and I wondered if perhaps a party at home would have been better.

I regretted choosing the party. It had been an horrendous day and I was so upset. I cried all day Sunday with the memory of it. No one and nothing could console me. As if to make up for the disappointing and distressing day, my parents bought me a Kodak camera for a present the following week. It served me well for years but was a constant reminder of that dreadful day.

The one good thing to come from being 21 was that I decided it was time to pay for my board. Mum gave me a good grilling in an effort to make sure I knew about all the expenses that would be required and my responsibilities,

The camera Valerie received for her 21st birthday. (V. Tedder)

123

before we agreed on a sum to be paid every Friday night without fail. No way was she going to subsidise me when on sick leave or unemployed. Hastily I agreed that I had taken all her arguments into consideration and would uphold my obligations.

I found that it was not easy to keep within my allowance. For the first time in my life I began to realise just how much things cost and how much Mum spent on items like toiletries, shoe repairs, clothes and miscellaneous essentials that I had taken for granted. Although it meant I had more money, spending it on luxuries such as the cinema meant that cosmetics and social events had to take a back step. I chose my own clothes and shoes, but walked the shops for the best bargains and always with one thought in mind. Would they be serviceable and last? There was no extra cash for the purchase of frivolous garments or silly styled shoes. However, I enjoyed the freedom of spending my own well earned money and it taught me to be thrifty and sensible. Saving for holidays and those special items and events made it more of a pleasure when the time came to enjoy the fruits of such sacrifices.

When I reflect on those years between 15 and 21, when Mum had all my wages except for some spending money, she served me well. I was always well dressed, usually in the height of fashion, and my requests for cosmetics and other sundries were frequently provided. I don't recall going without much and there was always a little extra in clothes and money when holiday time came around. I think she gave me a good grounding when it came to money matters and to being independent. Never did I ask my parents for money when I started paying my way. Mum was strict enough to refuse and I was well aware of her thoughts on the subject of lending or borrowing cash. In fact, my parents were never well off and I would not have dreamed of asking them for money, so I made certain that if I wanted something, I saved for it first.

A decision that changed my life

All was well at the Trafford in 1955. Full employment, good workmates, machining along to music while we worked, and a reasonable wage at the end of the week. Then came a rumour. It was something I could never have dreamt would happen. If it occurred, all my ambition to be a sample hand was doomed.

The rumour, that Ladies Pride Fashions was moving from Lancaster Street to premises on the Abbey Lane on the other side of the city, was rather a bombshell. It spread like wildfire through the firm and we started wondering about our jobs. The rumour ran for several weeks and despite questioning the management, they were reluctant to allay our fears with any useful information. It was all secret negotiations and speculation among the workforce ran high.

Eventually the rumour became fact. No official notice was posted but a verbal statement was given to us by the forelady. Basically, she indicated that at some date in the future Ladies Pride would be moving to new premises on Abbey Lane. Our jobs were safe if we were prepared to transfer. It seemed a long way from Lancaster Street to Abbey Lane.

For days I discussed the move and its possibilities. Mum, as practical as ever, pointed out that in addition to the extra travelling time, morning and night, it would mean two buses there and back daily. Money for fares would have to be found. There was no getting home for lunch. This could be purchased from the canteen or I would have to take a packed lunch. Either way it meant more expense with no increase in wages. I was working flat out to earn four to five pounds a week as it was.

Mum advised me to look for another job and not to wait until moving day. Similar firms in the district were advertising for experienced lockstitch machinists and overlockers and I should have no difficulty in obtaining a job. It was a busy time of the year getting the autumn and winter garments onto the market. Prospects of suitable work was good and I stood a better chance of a good job by taking the initiative before being forced to do so.

It took me quite a time to come to terms with the fact that it would be totally uneconomical for me to make the transfer on my wages. My days at the Trafford were numbered. My ambitions in the trade were to come to nothing after all and I was destined to start again elsewhere. I decided to stick it out as long as possible. Then one day the news spread among the workforce that the transfer date was two months ahead. Mum said I was not to wait and to look for other employment. Within a few days I secured a similar job as a dressmaker for a firm named Benson in Linden Street, just a ten minute walk from home. I was not sure whether it was the right job at the time but it was to be a change from making up ladies' suits and dresses. It meant that I should not keep abreast of the latest fashions but learn how to make up children's and ladies' night attire, fancy blouses and celaneze [artificial silk] dresses. They made up a varied array of woollen garments. Being an experienced overlocker, I was promised work in this field when the trade fluctuated with the seasons. Nowhere was there a chance to become a sample hand or to better myself. I put this ambitious thought out of my mind.

I gave one week's notice at the Trafford. The forelady understood my decision and was very kind. My workmates were sad to see me leave on the Friday night and I was very upset because I did not want to leave. After six years I dreaded the thought of having to start again. As I left the firm I reflected on that year. It was still the year of my 21st birthday and I felt life had dealt me a cruel blow.

Benson's factory was totally different from my previous firm. The workroom was extremely large and everything was made up and dispatched from one room. It had a high ceiling with a glass roof that did nothing to keep us cool in the summer and warm in the winter. It was at this firm that I first learned there were extremes of heat and cold that workers could endure before walking out without getting the sack. I recall it was so cold one day that I machined in my top coat and boots before the management released us for the day. The heating was not as it should have been. It was nice to go home early and get warm, but there were no wages to cover that half day.

The forelady was small, slim and sullen looking. She had thin grey hair and wore spectacles. Everything she was involved in was usually required yesterday. Laughter was curbed when she was in the vicinity. She seemed to think us incapable of working and laughing at the same time. She bossed us and busied herself around us, and gave the impression that if she were not there the firm would close down. I learned to keep out of her way and my head bent low over the machine when she appeared on the scene.

My heart was not in the job though I worked the same hours and even accepted overtime when requested, money was money after all. But the work was so different and I began to find it harder to make a living. The rate of pay sounded good when I accepted the job, but I found out later that it was lower overall and the bonuses a lot less than anticipated. When I complained to the other women I was given the cold shoulder. The long stayers at the firm thought the pay was good but my experience at the Trafford had taught me otherwise. The Trafford rates were set by the Hosiery Union but Benson's rates came under a Dressmaking Federation with a totally different scale of pay. I began to have second thoughts about the trade unions. Nevertheless, there was no short time at Benson's so I knuckled down hoping for the best. I was optimistic something better would come along.

My time at Benson's passed without incident. There were no particular friends either among the workforce or outside factory hours. I was fully employed with lots of overtime and I managed to extend my skills on the machine to include overlocking, hemming and buttonholing. My heart was not in the job as I continued to machine away from 8am to 6pm Monday to Friday. Everyone was serious and to my dismay there was a lack of fun and laughter, something I had been used to. There was no music to machine along with or sing or whistle to as we worked, and for fifteen months life appeared very dull.

Just before Christmas 1956, a story spread through the factory that Rudkin and Laundon's, a similar knitwear factory to the Trafford and situated on St Saviour's Road, were advertising for lockstitch machinists. I saw a chance of a return to making up ladies' fashion garments again, and thoughts of renewing steps to be a sample hand began to collect in my mind. I decided to make enquiries.

Next day, full of confidence, I spent my lunch hour visiting the factory obtaining details of the work. I discovered to my pleasure that the foreman was keen to engage me when he heard of my previous experience and good apprenticeships with Martha Hill's and the Trafford. He was helpful and considerate. The rate of pay was similar to what I received at The Trafford and meant a small rise in my weekly wage. He was prepared to hold the job for me

while I worked out my two weeks' notice at Benson's. A date was fixed for me to start after the Christmas holiday.

Elated with joy at the prospects of a move and to start afresh, I returned to Benson's and gave the forelady my notice. She seemed to take it as a personal insult and was extremely angry. She lectured me and said I did not know when I was well off. Insisting that she accepted my notice, I gave her the date when I would be leaving and requested that my National Insurance Card and wages due to me were to be available on that day.

I worked hard during that first week of notice in an atmosphere that was indeed hostile. I ignored the sarcastic remarks from the forelady and from some of the long serving, married women on the bench. They could not understand that I was unhappy and I could not understand their attitude. They saw nothing wrong with the pay scales or the workings of the factory. They thought it one of the best firms in town to work for. Why did I want to leave?

It seemed that I was being very disloyal to the firm and was branded a troublemaker. I was selfish enough not to care. Then unfortunately I caught the flu. It was the second week of my notice and the doctor issued me with an official sick certificate. Because of the illness I was unable to collect my card and wages on the Friday as arranged. It meant leaving them until after the Christmas period. As soon as the factory opened again I went along to collect what was due to me. The forelady refused to hand them over. She stated quite firmly that I had not worked the second week of the notice period and I owed them a full week's work. Sick leave did not count and was unacceptable to the firm. We argued, but no matter what I said she would not budge and refused to hand over what was due to me. I threatened to sue her and the firm and left the premises. I was completely floored by her attitude but knew that without my card the job at Rudkin and Laundon's was in jeopardy.

Not knowing what rights the forelady had in withholding my card and wages, I sought the advice of my parents. Dad came to the rescue. That night we returned to Benson's and he waited outside the factory offices, in the street, while I attempted for a second time to collect what was due. He intended only to enter the factory if there was trouble.

My second attempt was no better than the first. The forelady was aggressive, abusive and flatly refused to hand over my documents and pay. I refused to argue any further. Leaving the factory floor, I made my way upstairs to the office manager. He was like a god at this firm and hardly ever showed his face on the factory floor where we worked. The forelady stormed behind me. The receptionist showed me into a small sales office while she contacted the manager, and the forelady continued her verbal abuse. While in the sales office she must have looked down into the street from one of the windows in the office because, suddenly, she rounded on me shrieking at the top of her voice that I was a troublemaker who had brought a boyfriend along as a threat. I protested, informing her he was my father and if she did not comply with my request he would come in and sort her out. She did not believe me and said so, but she flounced across the room to a small desk, threw open the drawer and pulled out my card and wage packet. She threw them across the desk at me saying that my name would be put on a black list and I would never be employed by the firm again. Good I thought, grabbing my card and wage packet and running from the room.

The unpleasant business troubled me for a time but I was glad to be rid of the firm and everyone in it. So on the following Monday morning I started work at Rudkin and Laundon's without a hitch. Immediately I was welcomed into the fold and the atmosphere was as different again. My sewing machine, in tiptop condition, was situated at the end of a bench of girls, all about my age. They were only too pleased to show me the ropes and assist with the work routine. The foreman, an elderly man, was charming and efficient and went out of his way to make everything run smoothly. He fancied himself as a dad fussing over his young ladies. Quickly settling down, I soon forgot about the previous hard working. and unfriendly fifteen months and began to earn approximately five pounds and ten shillings a week on a regular basis. This was a good wage in 1957.

Despite working once again in a happy atmosphere with extremely jovial workmates, an uneasiness spread over me and I was not totally satisfied with my lot. Gradually I saw there was no chance of improving or advancing my occupation and dreams of becoming a sample hand were gone. Two attractive and very fit young women were handling the job surprisingly well and there was no hope of me, a newcomer to the firm, squeezing one of them out.

It seemed I was destined to be a machinist all my life and it went very much against my feelings. I felt I could become someone better in a more satisfying job.

The routine work and boredom, together with little social life, began to take its toll and I withdrew into myself, becoming more depressed and quiet as the weeks went by. Thoughts of a complete change of occupation began to grow and I frantically searched the local press for work of a different nature. Not being particularly advanced in education, coupled with the fact that after eight years in factories working with my hands and not much brain power, there seemed little scope. Inwardly I knew I was capable of better things if given a chance. But at what?

Then one day in October 1957 I found the answer. It was my practice every Saturday afternoon to travel into the city centre to purchase the weekend greengrocery from the retail market. On one of these shopping expeditions, and during a very heavy shower of rain, I sheltered in a shop doorway near to the Clock Tower. Sharing the small dry space was a tall, smart and efficient looking policewoman. I stood entranced for quite some time watching her deal with the members of the public. I was full of admiration at her coolness and confidence and began to wonder if I could do such a job. The policewoman was a rare sight on the streets of Leicester and the small band of female officers I had seen were very much admired and respected.

Gradually it dawned on me that I might be capable of this work and spent the rest of the afternoon deciding whether to apply or not. The more I thought about it the more I liked the idea. It would be a far more interesting job and never boring. The qualifications were the problem - leaving school in 1949 with none to mention was a definite drawback. I had plenty of common sense and a little knowledge of what life was all about. My tutors in the factories were outspoken and I thought I knew a thing or two.

That night as I lay in bed, I made up my mind. Nothing ventured, nothing gained. I had no doubt it was a career I wished to follow and, if accepted, I intended to make it a success. I made the decision not to tell the family of my plans.

The following Saturday morning I called in at Uppingham Road Police Station and obtained a number of pamphlets and an application form. The constable on the enquiry desk telephoned Charles Street Police Station and arranged an appointment for an interview the following Saturday. I decided to make all the arrangements for visits or any telephone communications for Saturdays. I could not afford to loose pay taking time off from work. In addition I did not want anyone at the factory knowing my plans. It was my secret. If I was not accepted then no one would be the wiser.

I survived a very searching interview, the tough entrance examinations, the farce of a medical, the eyesight test and the intense scrutiny into my background, character and family.

It was a good job that when I had completed this list of requirements I told my parents of my intentions. A personal visit from the woman inspector to my home, vetting them and asking extremely personal questions about my behaviour and character made Mum begin to wonder what on earth her eldest daughter had been up to. It appeared that the inspector was keen to know, at the age of twenty three and still unmarried, whether I was joining the police force to catch a husband or if I was man mad. There was no place in the force for that type of woman. She had to be satisfied that I was joining for the right reasons and ready to accept a hard working career with very unsociable hours. The Police Committee were reluctant to employ women who were not prepared to give a lifetime of service.

Then the nail biting session began. During the next few days while I awaited their decision, I reflected on life at Nottingham Road. We still suffered the strange and obnoxious smells, the clogged up drains, the damp, the cold, the bales stored in the gateway, the mice and the cockroaches. Perhaps eventually in a new career I might be able to find a way of getting us out of Nottingham Road to a more pleasant property with a better environment. Maybe I was the one to get the breaks which would improve our standard of living. I wondered, would I have 'Technicolor' polka dots on my new white police shirts? And what would Mr Wilson have to say about that?

Everyday I checked the post. Then it arrived - an appointment to attend Charles Street Police Station the following Saturday morning. Feeling sick to my stomach with apprehension, I was greatly relieved and full of excitement when, on my arrival, the woman inspector informed me that I had been accepted. I could not believe my good fortune. My appointment to the Police Service was later verified by post giving me a starting date. Then and only then, was I to give notice to my employers.

The eagerly awaited letter arrived two days later. It gave me a starting date which would allow me to take two weeks' leave over the Christmas period and plenty of time to prepare and collect my uniform and sundries ready for the Police Training School at Mill Meece in Staffordshire. I wallowed in thoughts of having two week's holiday and went to work happy to give the required notice.

My work mates were taken by surprise and there was a great deal of leg-pulling. The foreman was as pleased as punch and felt very proud to have known me despite the fact that I still had to prove myself at the training school. There were a couple of cynical persons who refused to believe me and only accepted it when they saw me in uniform patrolling the city centre a few months later. They thought me too timid and reserved to be a police officer. I was quite upset by their remarks, but I knew what I was doing and time alone would prove them wrong. I was told quite frankly by one of the older women who worked on the large steam presses that I was only a factory girl who had illusions of grandeur. Where had I got the idea from that I could carry out the duties of a police officer, she was at a loss to think. I ignored her remark. I'll show her, I thought.

I spent a happy Christmas and a wonderful New Year's Eve. Everyone who knew my plans wished me good luck and gave me words of encouragement. My parents were behind me giving me support, and I did not regret for one moment the step I was taking. Suddenly I felt that an enormous burden had been lifted from my shoulders. I felt free. To begin a new life away from the humdrum boring days in the factory, a chance to be away from home for the first time in my life and be independent, to accept responsibilities and achieve something with my life gave me a great feeling of satisfaction. I did not envisage at the time the sort of adventures I would be involved in. Nor did I foresee the hazardous work, the sordid and distressing incidents and long hours that were in store for me in the future. I just saw a career so marvellous and different to anything I had ever dreamed of, and one that nobody knew very much about. I felt like a pioneer. It was still in the early days for women to be accepted into male dominated professions and I knew there would be many prejudices to overcome.

There was a time during the first few weeks as a police officer when an elderly retired constable took one look at me and said, 'You'll never last'. He thought me too young, reserved and naive. But I did last. Twenty six years and eight months to be exact. And that is another story.

Valerie at Mill Meece Police Training School, 1958 (V. Tedder)

By the same author

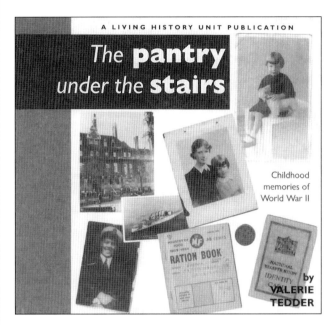

A LIVING HISTORY UNIT PUBLICATION

The **pantry** under the **stairs**

Childhood memories of World War II

by **VALERIE TEDDER**

"I was five years and two months old when the world was once again plunged into war. I sat on my Mother's lap at Grandma Howgill's house in Kate Street, Leicester, surrounded by uncles and aunts. Mother was the eldest of eight, having one sister, Edie, and six brothers. Aunt Annie, Grandma's spinster sister, fluttered about the room from one side to the other, wringing her hands in despair. We were gathered there to listen to a very important wireless announcement. "

This vivid account of a wartime childhood in and around Leicester will appeal to readers of all ages.

ISBN 0 9521090 1 8

£4.99

Other Living History publications:

Videos

Time of Our Lives (Leicester in the first half of this century) £12.99
Talk of the Town (Leicester in the 1950s and '60s) £13.50
Leicester on Parade (Leicester takes to the streets 1930s - 1960s) £13.50

Books

The Diary of Ada Jackson 1883 £5.99
(also available on audio tape as a talking book £7.99)
Highfield Rangers: An Oral History £4.99
Out and About in Leicester £5.99
On the Starting Line - a history of athletics in Leicester £6.99
The Pantry Under the Stairs - childhood memories of World War II £4.99
(also available on audio tape as a talking book £9.50)
Wharf Street Revisited £6.50
A Leicester Calendar - 365 dates in the history of Leicester £2.50
Leicester Celebrates - festivals in Leicester past and present £6.50
Parampara - 30 years of Indian music and dance in Leicester £3.50
A Guide to Sources for Local History (spiral bound) £9.00
Desirable Locations - Leicester's middle class suburbs 1880-1920 £7.00
All Part of the Service - a pictorial history of Leicester's service industries £6.00
The Story of the Saff - a history of the Saffron Lane Estate £6.50
In Sickness and in Health - a history of Leicester's health and ill-health 1900-1950 £7.50